VISIONARY TRIBUTES

"The resonance I feel with Damanhur and the mission of The Oracle Institute fills me with passionate promise for the future of the human race. Coherence of this magnitude is a clear indication of a deep pattern within the universe, and it is the same force which guides my work at the Foundation for Conscious Evolution, The Shift Network, and with colleagues throughout the world."

~ **Barbara Marx Hubbard**, co-founder of the Foundation for Conscious Evolution; global ambassador for The Shift Network; member of the Evolutionary Leaders Group, World Future Society, and Assoc. for Global New Thought; and author of *The Hunger of Eve*, *Emergence: The Shift from Ego to Essence*, and *Birth 2012 and Beyond*

"The Damanhur community is a truly paradigm-expanding experiment in conscious living. Its design, evolution, and artistry are a testament to the unique genius of Falco – an evolutionary pioneer."

~ **Stephen Dinan, M.A.**, founder and CEO of The Shift Network; member of the Evolutionary Leaders Group; and author of *Radical Shift: Spiritual Writings from the Voices of Tomorrow* and *Sacred America: Fulfilling Our Country's Promise* with Marianne Williamson

"Here is the revelation of the soul of a mystery school, that once and future experience of exploring the ways in which the self is put into service for the SELF ... and the world mind grows as a consequence."

~ **Jean Houston, Ph.D.**, founder of The Foundation for Mind Research, Renaissance of Spirit Mystery School, and the Jean Houston Foundation for social artistry; global advisor on human development to the United Nations and UNICEF; and author of *A Passion for the Possible*, *A Mythic Life*, and *The Wizard of Us*

"These books are a poetic tribute to the Absolute bearing witness to its own creation through the eyes of a deeply inspired mystic."

~ **Andrew Cohen**, spiritual teacher and founder of EnlightenNext; and author of *My Master Is My Self*, *Embracing Heaven & Earth*, and *Evolutionary Enlightenment* with Deepak Chopra

"History hinges on the lives and actions of great individuals. Building the Temples of Humankind was a mission from a higher spiritual world. Falco has inspired a community to bring heaven to earth."

> ~ **Alex Grey and Allyson Grey, M.F.A,** founders of the Chapel of Sacred Mirrors (CoSM), a sanctuary for encouraging the creative spirit; publishers of *Damanhur: Temples of Humankind,* and Alex is Chair of the Sacred Art Department at Wisdom University and author of *Sacred Mirrors, The Mission of Art,* and *Net of Being*

"Falco is an explorer at the frontiers of the human experience. He sees what others only intuit, and he thereby provides insight into the potential for the human future in that domain of our identity where there are at present deep yearnings but no maps."

> ~ **Jim Garrison, Ph.D.,** founder and CEO of Ubiquity University; founder of Wisdom University and The State of the World Forum; and author of *America As Empire, Civilization and The Transformation of Power,* and *Climate Change and the Primordial Mind*

"This look into the personal perspectives of Falco – a living Avatar – is a poetic walk through the internal work and wisdom of one who has brought us astonishing beauty and creativity. You'll find practical wisdom interwoven with cosmic musings that result in a provocative and enlightening window into the mind of a very special man."

> ~ **John L. Petersen,** futurist and founder of The Arlington Institute; author of *A Vision for 2012: Planning for Extraordinary Change* and *Out of the Blue: How to Anticipate Big Future Surprises;* and publisher of the e-newsletter *FUTUREdition*

"The *Three Books of the Initiate* are uniquely different than any other spiritual books on the market today – and I do mean unique. They read as if Oberto were interpreting my third near-death experience, seeing what I saw, feeling what I felt, lending heft to that sense of Presence when you truly become one with The One. The texts stretch thought about who we are, where we came from, and why we're here. The books are stunningly powerful."

> ~ **P.M.H. Atwater, L.H.D.,** researcher of near-death and evolutionary states; and author of *The Real Truth About Death, Children of the Fifth World, Beyond the Indigo Children, Future Memory,* and *Near-Death Experiences: The Rest of the Story*

DYING TO LEARN

First Book of the Initiate

OBERTO *"Falco"* AIRAUDI

WITH A FOREWORD BY LAUREL OF *The Oracle Institute*

Translated by Elaine Baxendale
Edited by Silvia *"Esperide Ananas"* Buffagni

Published by The Oracle Institute Press, LLC

A division of The Oracle Institute, a 501(c)(3) educational charity
1990 Battlefield Drive
Independence, Virginia 24348
www.TheOracleInstitute.org

Copyright © 2012 by Oberto Airaudi

Revised English Edition

Publisher's Cataloging-in-Publication Data

Airaudi, Oberto.
  Dying to learn / Oberto "Falco" Airaudi ; with a
foreword by Laurel of the Oracle Institute ; translated
by Elaine Baxendale ; edited by Silvia Buffagni. -- Rev.
English ed.
  p. cm. -- (First book of the Initiate)
  LCCN 2012941974
  ISBN 978-1-937465-01-8

  1. End of the world--Fiction. 2. Messiah--Fiction.
3. Human-alien encounters--Fiction. 4. Science fiction.
I. Baxendale, Elaine. II. Title. III. Series: Airaudi,
Oberto. Initiate ; 1st bk.

PS3601.I78D95 2012   813'.6
                           QBI12-600175

Cover and book design by Donna Montgomery
Printed in the United States

CONTENTS

FOREWORD

Laurel of The Oracle Institute

The largest full moon of the year awakens me this morning. Glowing white light hits the New River, the oldest river in America, and bounces through my bedroom window, calling me outside. I am surprised by its magnetism. The moon pulls me out of bed, as surely as it pulls the blood from my body, perhaps for the last time. I am fifty now and acutely aware of the cycles of life.

I stand in the moonlight with Shadow, my canine companion for the past fourteen years. He lifts his nose into the misty atmosphere of the Virginia Highlands, the Appalachian vista where The Oracle Institute is located, so similar to the Italian Alps which cradle and protect the Federation of Damanhur.

Shadow is smelling the moonbeams. The mystery of the moon is speaking to us both, and I cherish the moment. Shadow will not be with me much longer; he is old now and lame in his hind quarters. My mind and my heart make note of this precious, passing time with such a noble creature. And I am reminded that in Damanhur, residents take the name of an animal and plant at their initiation.

Then suddenly, I am transported back in time five years. My being shifts to the Valchiusella Valley in Italy, where I spent three brief but glorious days. Now, instead of the New River, I am staring at the Chiusella River, which winds its way alongside Damanhur. Magical memories flood me ... as the messages contained in the *Three Books of the Initiate* will flood you.

The trip to Damanhur changed my life, or rather, my perspective on life. I first learned of Damanhur in a 2007 issue of *What Is Enlightenment?* magazine, published by Andrew Cohen of EnlightenNext, a non-profit teaching center in Massachusetts and compatriot of Damanhur in building the New World. EnlightenNext had dedicated this issue to mankind's changing views on "Utopia," starting with the biblical belief that we must die in order to reach "Heaven." Hardly the cycle of rebirth and learning we will contemplate in the *Initiate* series.

The EnlightenNext article then discussed the next stage of our utopian yearning - the Age of Reason - during which Sir Francis Bacon wrote a futuristic novella entitled *The New Atlantis* (1624). This book describes a sanctuary known as the "College of the Six Days" (i.e., of creation), a no-war zone where the best and brightest achievements of humanity would be stored, cherished, and enhanced. Thus, humanity began to imagine "Heaven on Earth," a major step forward in our psycho-spiritual development.

Lastly, the EnlightenNext article described modern views on Utopia, including Teilhard de Chardinís concept of the "Noosphere," a theoretical bubble of consciousness that surrounds our planet and expands as the collective consciousness grows. The Noosphere is similar to the "Akashic" field and the "Universal One" described by American mystics Edgar Cayce and Walter Russell. Long known to the mystics of Hinduism and Buddhism, this ethereal region is a state of mind which is available once we commit to the quest for enlightenment. Its discovery allows for spectacular spiritual ascension in the current life, such that the life-death-life cycle is "broken." If still questioning the possibility of rebirth, readers may wish to peruse the research of Ian Stevenson, Ph.D., former head of the psychiatry department at the University of Virginia. Over the span of forty years, Dr. Stevenson compiled more than 3,000 case studies on reincarnation.

Undoubtedly, Jesus made contact with the Noosphere (a/k/a God). And Jesus explained this state of awareness in the *Gospel of Thomas*, which some scholars believe predates the *Gospels of Mark* and *Matthew*.

> *Whoever finds the interpretation of these sayings will not experience death. ...*
>
> *Let him who seeks continue seeking until he finds. When he finds, he will become troubled. When he becomes troubled, he will be astonished, and he will rule over the all. ...*
>
> *If those who lead you say, "See, the kingdom is in the sky," then the birds of the sky will precede you. If they say, "It is in the sea," then the fish will precede you. Rather, the kingdom is inside of you, and it is outside of you. When you come to know yourselves, then you will become known, and you will realize that it is you who are the sons of the living Father.*

Gospel of Thomas, Verses 1 - 3

Sadly, the true teachings of Jesus were purposely suppressed by men of power. In 450 C.E., Pope Leo I ordered that the apocryphal gospels "should not only be forbidden, but entirely destroyed and burned with fire."

Thereafter, the Reformation Movement, in an attempt to stem the Vatican's corruption, merely compounded the spiritual confusion. Today, orthodox Christianity and its stepchild Evangelicalism have spawned a new round of theosophical errors. Indeed, a passage in *Dying to Learn* speaks to the bastardization of Christ's mission, as our hero OroCritshna explains:

> *My playmate of two thousand years ago insists he wants to renew things. Even though his very name has been used to keep them as they are!*

So who exactly is Falco and why would you want to read his *Three Books of the Initiate*? Falco is the founder of Damanhur, which EnlightenNext voted the most utopian community on the planet. In addition, Damanhur has been recognized by the United Nations as a sterling example of how humanity may live compassionately and sustainably.

At present, Damanhur is home to approximately one thousand people, who live communally and operate roughly eighty cooperative businesses. Damanhur has its own Constitution, which governs the internal operations of the community as democratically decided upon by the residents. Damanhur also has its own micro-currency, school system, medical facilities, and media network. And all residents help build the Temples to Humanity, an underground complex of sacred spaces dedicated to our evolving consciousness and concepts of God. These temples repeatedly have been described as the "Eighth Wonder of the World."

When I visited Damanhur with my family, my delight actually was eclipsed by the awe I saw in my children's eyes. Yes, they were hugely impressed with the Coliseum in Rome, a gondola ride in Venice, and Michelangelo's statue of David in Florence. However, they were overwhelmed by Damanhur. My youngest son compared it to Hogwarts, as we passed through concealed hallways and descended hidden staircases. And my mother remarked, "The Damanhur temples rival the Egyptian pyramids! How did they do it?"

In secret. They built the temples in secret, with no construction permits, no architects or engineers, and no heavy equipment. In fact, there is a museum at Damanhur that showcases how they built their subterranean complex: pictures of men and women wearing hard-hats and armed with flashlights, pick-axes, and buckets. Truly, the Temples to Humanity must be seen to be believed.

After building in secret for over a dozen years, the Damanhurians received an unexpected visit from the Italian police, who in 1991 swooped down by helicopter to investigate. As the story goes, Falco calmly invited the officials into the temples. An hour later, the police emerged with tears in their eyes, vowing to help Falco make it "legal." Five years later in 1996, the Italian government granted the necessary permits, and since then the public has been invited to tour the Temples to Humanity.

In short, the success of Damanhur is unparalleled. No intentional community in the United States comes close to matching Damanhur's level of environmental sustainability and spiritual commitment. Ambassadors from Damanhur will visit The Oracle Institute this year for the fourth time, to further share Damanhurian philosophies and to advise us on how to build our own unique community in Independence, Virginia. Consequently, I have had ample opportunity over the years to ask questions about the Damanhur lifestyle and the many rumors that circulate on the internet about Falco ...

Probably the best way to summarize the Damanhur experience is to compare it to indigenous native cultures. Damanhurians honor the web of life, the symbiotic nature of our co-existence with the planet, and the cycle of rebirth. Compare this philosophy with that of the Native Americans:

> *Every part of this soil is sacred in the estimation of my people. ... And when the last Red Man shall have perished, and the memory of my tribe shall have become a myth among the White Men, these shores will swarm with the invisible dead of my tribe .... The White Men will never be alone.*
>
> *[B]e just and deal kindly with my people, for the dead are not powerless. Dead, did I say? There is no death, only a change of worlds.*

Chief Seattle, Duwamish Tribe (1854)

Also like the native peoples, Damanhurians revere the Great Mystery and are encouraged to explore the origin of the Universe in their own way:

> *Brother ... we also have a religion which was given to our forefathers and has been handed down to us their children. ... It teaches us to be thankful for all the favors we receive; to love each other; and to be united. We never quarrel about religion. ...*
>
> *The Great Spirit does right; he knows what is best for his children; we are satisfied. Brother, we do not wish to destroy your religion, or take it from you; we only want to enjoy our own.*

Chief Red Jacket, Seneca Tribe (1805)

Thus, Damanhurians pursue various spiritual paths, such as the "Way of the Monks and Nuns," the "Way of the Word," and the "Way of the Oracle." Falco teaches that at this stage of our evolutionary journey, humans are a "bridge species," because we are on the cusp of defining and transcending into a new spiritual paradigm. He respects and honors the ancient traditions. In fact, one of the largest underground temples is dedicated to the numerous religions that mankind has fashioned since the dawn of time. Yet, Falco also believes that we are ready to adopt more sophisticated belief systems, in better keeping with our highest moral aspirations, greater historical perspective, and ever-increasing scientific comprehension of the Cosmos.

As for Falco himself: *He is the greatest mystery of all!* Rumors abound concerning his ability to see the future, access the Universal Mind, and even time travel. Clearly, Falco is one-of-a-kind, a true visionary who has co-created a stunning and resilient model for life in the New Millennium. Currently, he is working on his autobiography, in which he will share many (and hopefully all) of his secrets.

Falco is careful, though, not to encourage others to replicate the Damanhur experiment elsewhere. He wisely recognizes that every culture is different and, therefore, that every region of the world must craft an appropriate template of future co-existence based on local mores, geography, resources, and talents. In the New River Valley where Oracle is located, we hold a vision of developing a 21st Century community that is based on the Appalachian tradition. We call this the "Valley of Light" project.

In closing, I wish to underscore another of Falco's core teachings: *We are running out of time.* Currently, the old world is collapsing and few of us are prepared for the inevitable turbulence that will ensue. Falco wrote *Dying to Learn* to emphasize this inconvenient truth.

In the *First Book of the Initiate*, humanity has failed to timely manifest the New World and disaster has befallen our beloved planet. OroCritshna has been sent to earth – the latest in a long line of Avatars – to remind us, once again, of our Divine origin and Divine potential. Thus, *Dying to Learn* is a dire warning of an ugly, dystopian future ... but one that may be avoided if we act swiftly.

Which brings me to you, the reader: Are you concerned that the cycle of birth, death, rebirth, and learning may come to a grinding halt on planet earth? What are you doing, personally, to help manifest a more utopian future?

Tragically, scientists report that we are undergoing the "Sixth Great Extinction," which is quite different from the previous five extinction events: It is the first time that humans will be present during a mass loss of life. Additionally, many scientists assert that we are causing it! Please, do what you can to help your community and, as the Iroquois would say, the next seven generations. Let us not break the sacred life-death-life cycle, but our shameful cycle of greed, pride, and war. Surely, we now have the knowledge and power to consciously evolve into a higher state of being.

For our part, The Oracle Institute is building the "Peace Pentagon" along the banks of the New River, which will serve as our headquarters and as a multi-faith sanctuary for peace building and conflict transformation. Energetically, we intend to hold the Light in southern Virginia, in stark contrast to the energy being held by the more notorious Pentagon in northern Virginia.

Now, please clear your mind, choose your favorite reading spot, and enjoy the esoteric journey which follows, brought to us compliments of Falco from Damanhur.

Laurel

Laurel is the pen name of Reverend Laura M. George, J.D., the founder and Executive Director of The Oracle Institute, a charity dedicated to assisting humanity through the difficult transition into the New Millennium. Oracle operates an award-winning publishing house and a spirituality school, both of which promote interfaith understanding.

Laura is a former attorney and former Catholic, who spiritually awakened with the events of September 11, 2001. Thereafter, she quit the practice of law and started writing about the "Trickle-Down Deity Theory" and the dangers of religious fundamentalism, which she views as the single greatest threat to humanity's continued evolution.

In 2004, Laura started Oracle with a group of like-minded souls who believe that the world is on the verge of a major paradigm shift, the likes of which we have not seen since Jesus walked the earth. Today, Laura is a full-time charity coordinator, truth seeker, and social visionary.

In 2011, Laura became an ordained interfaith minister, and she oversees Oracle's multi-faith programs. She also oversees construction of the "Peace Pentagon," Oracle's new headquarters, retreat center, and sacred space in Independence, Virginia, along the New River, the oldest river in America and the second oldest river in the world.

Laura is the author of Oracle's award-winning trilogy: *The Truth: About the Five Primary Religions*; *The Love: Of the Fifth Spiritual Paradigm*; and *The Light: And the New Human.*

Laura has visited Damanhur and the Temples to Humankind, and she wishes to express her gratitude to Falco for choosing The Oracle Institute Press as his English representative.

PREAMBLE

*O*roCritshna is an Envoy; his duty is the purification and the liberation of Humankind. He descends one day, after a heavy thunderstorm, breaking up the black clouds and driving away the hail, into the midst of the despairing members of a Community arisen after the collapse of Industrial Civilization. The cities have been abandoned for some years, and pollution still continues to do damage.

By now cars are extremely rare, and many humans who believed in the myth of Consumerism have disappeared.

The present society is in a period of toil; the return to the earth is hard work but also the only way to survive.

The great, crazy dream of Waste is over, and many find themselves lost, disappointed and without ideals.

It is in this climate that the great Lords of Time, the Lords of Light, the Companions of the Universe who watch over the evolution of Humankind, send into the world a creature with MEMORY.

Yes, the extraordinary power of this being is not so much telekinesis, telepathy, or the ability to heal, but, rather, that of REMEMBERING. That part of reality that the ordinary man forgets – the dreams, the powers of everyone locked in the unconscious – are for the Envoy conscious. He knows, and he teaches.

So many stories are told about his coming, just as previously happened with the Buddha, with Christ, with Muhammad and other Masters.

More simply, perhaps, he is a normal person Born of Woman, whom the On High allowed to REMEMBER, and to narrate to men of "good will" that life is eternal, that the goal is evolution and purification and KNOWLEDGE, that Humankind can, if it wants, yet save itself and harmoniously save its own world.

Like the ancient philosophers before him, OroCritshna sits in the evenings around the fire among his fellow men, after they return from their hard work in the fields. As yet, the men do not consciously remember, so he recounts to them what each one, deep down, already knows.

Let us draw close and let us also listen. Who knows, one might become an Initiate.

He waits for us and speaks and writes … even for YOU.

PART ONE

I have been born so many times I have lost count. Even my awakening has passed through lives of preparation. In every continent and in my own way, it carries on even now. America in 1812, Europe a little earlier, Asia, ancient Africa, Europe again, and so on ...

By now, I am bored of being born.
I know the stars and the eras.
I have seen oak trees be born and die very old.
I have been leaf and fruit.
I have fed upon myself.
I have seen unthinkable heavens and suns.
I have thought unimaginable thoughts.
I have not breathed.
I have fished in rivers and I have been fished.
I have been Time.
I have forgotten my names and changed faces and voices.
I have had wounds, and I have died with battle companions for a thousand flags.
I am pen and paper, sword and side, diamond and coal.

I have learned to die in a hundred different schools, and I have died to learn, yet again, how to die.

Dying to learn.

The spirals have opened and closed again.[4]
Suns have grown cold and hair has changed color.
My tombs have been different: water, earth, fire and abandonment.
I have been my glittering prison.
My senses have been mutilated and widened.
I have had blindness and the sight of a falcon.

I believe I am a pentagram, and each life is a note.
I am learning, but still laziness files down my fingers.
I have done every job and spoken every language.
I have forgotten and found again.
I have loved beyond time and found my loves again.
I have searched for myself, loved myself, avenged and been grateful.

I have left indelible traces in every history of the world, until history itself has been forgotten.
The line of my hearts is long like the cobweb is to the spider.
I have had every fear; I am one who remembers.
I have seen the fixed stars shift in the sky, and I have heard the breath of God several times.
Am I ever happy? Oh, now I cannot forget how often I was ill.

---

[4] The galaxies, which indicate the flow of the great epochal cycles.

The woods and the seas are my dwelling place.

I have lived in millions of ravines. I have seen sea cliff rise and mountain chains disappear.

I have found my friends and my loves again.

I have been my shore and the river my time.

I have eaten all manner of things. I have melted rock and I have nourished myself with earth and with light. I have killed and devoured, captured and chased. I have been trapped and tortured.

Your silent glance tells me an infinity of things. Just as your eyes on these lines speak to me about you, while I tell you how I am and how you are.

My eternity has been uselessly devoured by time.

Light and darkness have quickly flashed like lightning over my head and beneath.

The most precious of jewels have I possessed and lost playing at dice or at war. And won and lost again.

I have chewed in hunger on my limbs to feel less pain.

I am older still every time, but learning, I become young again.

When I am wise I am poor, and rich for others.

When I am drunk, my mind, distorted, does not remember – selfish.

Every time I have learned to read and write again, I have made the same mistakes, then remember I had already made them.

I have bought and sold my life until I understood I am eternal. Then I have made a gift of my soul, without asking for anything in return.

I have painted on vases, hidden and found treasures again.

I have learned to think, every time giving thought a different value.

I have heard God laugh and I have laughed with him without understanding. I have desired to be his laughter, and I have been satisfied.[2]
have wanted to be God, and I have learned to laugh.
I have descended into hell. I have been all the demons and a friend of theirs, if ever a demon can have friends.
I have been a necklace, and every pearl was born from my oyster belly, and mine was the neck that wore me.

It is thought that the heavens are a lace cloth and every star a hole. Behind the stars there is a Shining God, and the light of the stars is his Light. For some, every life is a beautiful woman who brings you quivers and concerns. What you will do with it, you have done already so many times, but every time is a renewal of the ancient.

Pleasure is a state of Consciousness and a key word opens its windows: now to the North, the South, the East or the West. The landscape forever changes while remaining eternally the same.

Often I have seen the tombs where useless traces of me are preserved. And if I look at a calendar, perhaps one of those saints could be me.
But I don't celebrate my name.

Perhaps I knew how to sing, since I am so out of tune now. The birds used to come and listen, enchanted, and the

---

[2] The use of the masculine form for God is only a convention.

children would say: "Wh
    I don't need notes a
song, reciting it in minds

    It was courage that li
Divinity. Who was the first
    A work fixed in time: a r
made of stars to remind u_   _ _he task.
Now the same monument i_   _____ed with the Divinity.
    Is God his simulacrum? Or the veil? Or whoever lifts it?

During the hot summer, I dig my winter den or I hoe the earth. I sow and pull up the weeds because, sweating, I know the summer won't be long. But long will be the winter.

I have taken a handful of dry earth, and my sweat has turned it dark.

While I was looking at it, in my hand it broke open, and little, pointed, green leaves sprang up. It began to get heavy, while vine tendrils and flowers fought for space on my hand.

With this earth I shall feed my people!

The forest has enveloped me and given refuge to all the insects, and all the birds have found food. And all the goats and all the cows have fed their young on the grass from my handful of earth, grazing for hours on my hand.

My sweat has become a stream, the stream a river, and little by little, the valleys of my hand have filled up – lake and sea. The salty sweat has been host to millions of life forms. In the abysses, frightening battles between disturbing monsters have created the waves.

10 - Dying to Learn

The aura
The n

by ...

of my hand has become the atmosphere. Mountains have been climbed and time has gone a few minutes ... thousands and thousands of years. Taking a good look, I have seen myself in the centre of my hand holding a handful of earth.

I have forgotten everything that I was sure I would never forget.

What am I called? What is my name? And the sweet name of the person I love?

The Chinese say a woman's name is more beautiful if rich in vowels. Your name, my unknown love, is all the vowels ... whatever your name is.

But I cannot be yours, in that I do not possess myself.

I have forgotten what all the things are called, and I have made them mine.

With the same sounds, I call my legs and the trees, my hands and the birds of the air, the sun and every tiny living being.

It is easier to call you with my name, my friend. And if I shout your name everyone raises their head – men and women, hearing themselves called by name.

The key to my house opens all doors, but the lock of my house is opened only with this key.

Krishna says: "I am in all creatures but they are not in me."

The temples on the Nile and the statues have benevolently watched the water flow for thousands of years, and they have been submerged.

I have seen incredible, chiseled work being done with minuscule, perfect figures rich in expression. And when I raised my eyes to give my compliments to the artist, I realized the artisan was blind.

I have congratulated a hen because its egg was perfect, and it has looked at me without understanding.

I have heard a mother being complimented on having a beautiful baby say "Thank you!"

If my father had died before conceiving me, who would have been my father?

Once, a philosopher, an expert in magical sciences, decided to conceive himself. He loved a woman and when she fell pregnant by him, he died and incarnated in the fetus at the seventh month. Thus he was born, being conceived by himself, but the woman killed him after he was born. It was thus that he died twice to be born only once, and he learned double by dying for two.

Every true civilization is a thoroughbred horse: It gives you problems mounting it, but great satisfaction when it is yours. People get together in cities to feel more alone.

The mistrusting, thieving farmer no longer has neigbors to rob and commits suicide to steal his own life.

The artisan who knows everything about his own art dies without transmitting it to his unwilling apprentice. The weapons are sharp and shiny so that new rust has something to feed upon.

The book is bought not to be read but to be used as furniture. My body is the furniture of my thoughts. I live in myself and, at times, I am late in paying me the rent.

A work of art is one's own duty fulfilled.

For the soldier it is war, for the lover love.

If the others find you grown thin and tired, it is they who are tired and thin.

Creation is the fruit of its creatures.

An order is a deep desire, and a word of encouragement gives you incredible strength.

I have evoked an unnamable being of light and incredible power. It is not right to wonder if it is good or bad. I have opened the circle so it could come close to me or I could pounce on it.

It was afraid of me.

Fear is the circle that divides us. All of us.

Shy people suffer and sacrifice themselves for fear of the object of their shyness. That is how to pay a thousand times more for something than what it is worth.

Yesterday a desperate woman told me she is against abortion, and she is pregnant. She said she would kill herself by jumping from the roof. A child should be wanted and planned, of course, but sometimes it is the child's soul that makes the plans, and it is you who are born now or later.

A silly dog is no sillier than its owner, and in time, it can grow and show itself silently mature. It is the image that remains in our experience that shows us an immature reality.

A photograph tells me how you were, but also how you are. It is the difference between then and now that gives me an idea of you – what you have done, how you have used your talents.

A glass of pure crystal does not equal two hands cupped for sipping water at the spring. Similarly, your soul cannot be canned, any more than the moon. The words you express in prayer may never reach heaven, but in one instant your thoughts may create another moon.

If the puppy is crushed and dies, on another continent, its mother, asleep by the fire, lifts her head and pricks her ears whining. Like the moon, she hears without ears.

To those who dare ask, I cannot refuse what they want, if they are ready to pay. And if they are ready, I shall no longer ask the agreed price.

War distinguishes what is useful from what is useless. When death shall have come because every inch of my body has tried dying many times, I will die again and be renewed. And I shall be more eternal than ever.

I shall not die twice in the same manner. Few imaginable experiences are left for me now, even though human beings are always inventing new fantasies.

What shall I yet learn in this life? I have read papers I did not have the time to read before, and I have seen people from new perspectives by forgetting the past. Have I perchance married my father, given birth to my sister, or met my mother on the bus? It is possible. Everything is possible, even imagining poetry.

One day a God named Biologist placed in a circle a hundred insects – processionaries – which owe their name to the fact that they always follow the one in front by a few millimeters. Just outside the circle, the God placed some food, but the processionaries continued for days and days, with the light and with the dark, to follow each other, and languished with hunger.

Then a little processionary had an inspiration: She moved outward a little, just enough to let all of them find food.

I was thinking how, among the processionaries, the one who changed course must have been a giant of a thinker. Surely she will reincarnate in a higher form, while the Biologist takes her place.

It's been so long, in this life, since I've seen certain people that I'm almost convinced they are dead. And surely they think the same about me. Why, when we don't see someone for a while, do we have this thought?

I know that after one comes two and then three. I am acquainted with numbers and their relative value.

What is the point of counting if I already know the final number? And why does every figure that comes after every other one pigeonhole my mind and arrange my thoughts? Why then are events not to scale? Or is it only appearances? And if today were tomorrow and if yesterday had not aready gone by, where would I be right now?

The paths of eternity are many and it is easy to get lost. To be the shepherd of oneself sometimes is only presumption.

If I were grass, the world around me would be a thousand times faster. I would see branches and vine-tendrils moving swiftly, roots digging and breaking open the earth, plants wrestling for the light. But my present rhythm is that of a man, and the grass appears unmoving to me.

To me, the butterfly lives for a few hours when the sun comes up, and it will never see the stars and the night; its world is one solely of light. It will never understand the car that passes speedily by and runs it over in its wake. But it will ask itself and ask its God why this happened, and it will have an explanation that suits it, thought out and hence correct.

The fish caught by the bait does not understand why it is dying out of its world, but if it were swallowed by another sea creature it would know why. To die in air that burns you is something else. Your death is my happiness, and I hold in my hand, your body shiny with scales. You mirror me in your skin. Am I inside of you, repeated thousands and thousands of times, or outside of you?

I feed on your flesh because I must have life, and I throw away your bones so that you can have something back.

I have been born once again to learn some more. I also must teach and carry on the project that I have been over-seeing for centuries.

Do all prophets have a soul? Or is it just one soul in many bodies? The hand has touched your brow and you have become a whirling pinwheel of colors.

The high and the low are at your side. The skin melts and the blood can be seen in the veins, and beneath the veins, the organs pulsating. They have evaporated, and at last I can see your white bones – where a man and a woman are almost the same.

The potatoes will not have your manure this year.

And therefore, neither will you feed on them.

They will wait beneath the earth till you are reborn.

The people of antiquity traced lines and drawings many miles in length, but they are all part of the same design, and they join up and cross over to carry on in new forms. Even the wind has respected the thought of ancient man, while the new men destroy things they made themselves.

Forgetting is wise so as not to become proud if you were powerful, and so as not to take revenge if you were weak.

How many times have I spoken of the NOW!

But if I live what I say, every time is always and only the very first now ... and memory is useless.

I am a straw bag that can contain anything at all. I am full of bread and cheese, fruit and jewels. But I always remain a straw bag, if I don't want to lose myself.

And if I write, I am my ink. Yet my marks have no meaning for the ant that has to crawl over them in search of crumbs. Perhaps the ant also writes, with its dancing on the paper making no sense to me.

Your hair, my love, has every color I desire, because I don't love you for your hair. Your lips and your eyes are every shape I desire, and the same for your face and your body. I love you and I don't know your image, nor your hips, nor your hands. Who are you? When God separated us in creating us, we continued to search for each other.

When I notice I'm repeating the same identical gestures too many times, I observe myself with curiosity. How lazy are my mind and my body! Perhaps even our pursuit of each other is like the line of the processionaries, and the solution for both of us is not so far off.

In reality, we pursue each other in a dream where we never manage to see each other's face: "Who are you?" "What are you like?" "Are we each other's shadow?"

And if we are the same being, am I the right eye searching for you and the left is you searching for me? If I hug myself on my own, do I protect myself and make the fear and confusion go away?

Pain is my most beloved brother.[3]   He renews. I admire him. He often forces me to understand when my lazy mind sits down.

Do I love the essence of things or their image?

If you were old and falling apart, would I pull away from you in horror? And you, young and beautiful, would you draw near with love to my wrinkled, worn-out features?

Can tears rejuvenate your soul? And make you, thereby, myself?

Whatever is eternal does not grow old, of course. A diamond in the midst of a faded rose sparkles, just as it does among the petals of a fresh flower.

But it happens that fear shuts us in a corner.

Fear: the worst disease.

---

[3] In the Damanhur philosophy of life, the spiritual path is described as a "Path of Joy" - joy as a product of understanding and awareness. *Dying to Learn* represents the evolution of the soul from one life to the next, but it is also an allegory of the transformation of the self that leads to renewal, to re-birth during this lifetime. Changing one's way of thinking or opening up may be difficult, even painful at times, but only if one chooses it to be. Otherwise, with readiness and a sense of humor, it is possible to go beyond, to overcome fear, to defeat pain, and with some effort, overcome the limits of ego.

What would he say now, a Master who had to lead the peoples of the world forward? Would he speak of his own fear and ask for the bitter chalice of sacrifice to be taken from him?

Thus I envision a speech or a mental letter that he would deliver to the Companions of the Universe.

Letter to the Council

I am embittered.

*By the obtuseness of people's minds, by the glances
that seem to understand and do not understand,
by everyone's mental exaggerations.*

*Every speech is beautiful and has a hold on the heart of
the listener, but the words are sounds dumb of meaning.
Words ... but who digs for the vein of Truth?*

*Everybody asks – even as I am saying
something important – for a personal favor.
Magicians raised in pens? Not even.
Dare I declare that "we know WHO" was right? Is right?
That it is not worth bringing humans into the Brotherhood?*

*When I took on this commission (some of you were not in
agreement), I said that it was worth trying to save them.
Every day, do I perhaps try to hide the Truth from myself?*

*When they speak to me – and ask – I smile.
Who understands what I keep in the depths of my eyes?
That everything I give, I take away from myself?
Who understands their own evil (and pain)
and draws teaching from it?*

"Take it away, you take it away, I shall be grateful to you."
I take it away; I take it upon myself.
And physical life slips me by.
Those who are healed forget – immediately.
And with the first thing I do to correct or teach them,
they will then, presumptuously, stab me in the back.

They happily justify one another and
condemn each other without mercy.
Ego flares up more than ever.
False ideals flutter above them.
Blame is outside themselves.
Help them, Companions in the Battles of Chaos
and Brothers of Eden.

The sword of fire that first drove them out now calls them
back, and they do not understand.
Everyone believes that their own little tin box,
full of stones, shells and string,
contains the treasures of the world.
They refuse to free their hands to take a casket
of gold and jewels.

Why, brothers, do their minds close to the Truth!
Where is the race that endures such sacrifice,
that searches in pain for freedom?
Why is torture accepted when it achieves nothing, and
fear of death and suffering are prolonged by this dread.

Many times, behind my reassuring smile,
I have seen and ignored meanness and pettiness.
And yet you know my strength!

Who threw open the doors of the ancient city?
Who defeated the red army armed with iron?
Who opened the mountain and created two from it?
And how many of you, in your worlds, did I help to ascend?
I too have been helped – certainly.
But the help was always a thorn.
One does not throw a rope or a rope-bridge to help
whoever is initiated into the mysteries cross a ravine.
Rather, one throws a cable of thorns and poison.

Today they say that function creates the organ, but what
organ is created in those who refuse pain and effort?
I am tempted to pack my bags and return among you,
but I love even these wretches.
And to think that they do not want Grace,
they ignore it and refuse it.

One of them even offered to help me!
This idea moved me:
A woman who wanted to help me, and did not dare tell me!
When anyone asks, I give.

Time flows and the eternal never pauses.
What a strange planet!
Thinking of its ancient greatness, and seeing its heirs,
I feel a knot in my throat.
Can there rise from them, one day, the race and the mind
that can cry: "Present!" to the primordial Council?

What condemnation and what torture do the people of
this world consciously inflict upon themselves in order
to close their minds so much?

"Brothers!" – I cry – "The intoxication has ended,
and I cast aside the drugged wine!
Why do you continue your pretence of inebriation?
It is over, I tell you, and every chain torn asunder.
Why therefore do you hold your hands
as if they were still bound?"

I have received a reply to these thoughts of mine.
Now you encourage me (in a human way!),
even those of you who were against my project!
After all, all of us who in the past have done years
of "flight" over this material planet desire,
in spite of everything, to save its races.

My playmate of two thousand years ago insists
he wants to renew things.
Even though his very name has been used
to keep them as they are!

Fine.
I shall see what I can still do … with the
maximum possible Indifference and the maximum Love.
But I shall shorten the carriages on the train
so that it goes faster.
Do I return among you soon, or do I remain?
And if I remain, what for?

The children of blame accuse and remain children,
but the good father knows how to use justice.
Is it any use shouting, getting angry,
if they do not understand?
If I raise my voice, do they understand any better?

Your Council says to me:
"Stop them; let the impurities be decanted and deposited.
To separate the carriages, it is well worth the trouble of
stopping the train – so as to gather speed to go uphill,
but with a few less carriages.
Is this the reason, then, that you refuse to make stops?
So that everyone might continue together?"

Is it worth it? I do not know.
To know, I have to stop.
Or let go of those who cannot follow me and
arrive at the finishing post with one person … or alone.

It does not matter.
The work, this time too,
will be carried through to the end.

As always,

OroChritshna

PART TWO

Obedience to the Divine Order, therefore. But at times the scent you wear is annoying to others and suffocates them, until they get used to your atmosphere. Just because I live on cicadas and like them, I cannot pretend they are your favorite food. But if I know there will be nothing other than cicadas, then I'll try to teach you to live on them.

The heat of summer melts my thoughts, and the winter cold freezes them. The renewal of death gets rid of the clutter and frees the attic; it puts the house in order and does the big spring-cleaning. I am ready to face another life.[4]

I have lit a fire in the woods to call the nature spirits. I have shown them I can control it, keep it lit without risk, and stamp it out. Under the full moon they came into the clearing, free of shadows but for the grassy images magnified by the fire.

---

[4] With reference to the present incarnation.

They recognize me, and dancing swift below my knees, they make circles and patterns on the turf. Their seemingly senseless fooling around reminds me how our present life is peopled by ever more crazy gnomes.

The renunciation of living a life as one's own personal choice shows just how limited the moral development of this age is. Prisoners of ourselves.

I am an eight year old child, and I am three or four times older than that. But I always behave by running off like an eight year old, by being presumptuous or pushy like an eight year old, a braggart and a liar.

The lie comes from fear of telling the Truth: it seems banal but it is not. The more a man grows, the more sincere he should be.

There are moments when you feel strong, and weakness is a long way off.

While I am dancing and the music blares, I know that in the house next door, silent suffering slits the throat of someone who is dying.

To know the hour of your own death is not so terrible as it seems. You know how near your liberation is. To die singing. To feel nothing but bliss and bursting happiness. Elevation and liberation.

Your body stretches away and your soul blossoms.

I have seen the faces of many stare at me from their mournful photographs. I know far more about them than their relatives. I have accompanied them in death from one solstice to another. They are looking, smiling over my shoulder at what I am writing. And whoever loved you is reading with you ... you who are reading these lines.

The dates are flashes of Consciousness in the darkness of Infinity. As if every incarnation were a frame from the film of our real life.

The smells remind you that things exist. The flavor of a life reminds you of the others and your eternity.

A date that reminds me of joy recalls sorrow to you.

I cannot tell you of the wonders of that day if, for you, it is marred by the memory of sorrow.

I have in my head the memory of a guitar. Its sound has always stirred me and filled me with shivers. I climbed upon its chords and swam in its notes.

I have re-read my diaries of the same day years ago, and the effect is the same.

Those who accompanied me are no longer.

My travelling companions got off at the small stations, and concluded thus our meeting. Every time you turn around, someone is missing. Often without saying goodbye.

We are school friends, in the same great school of the earth, and we go to different classes. Some move up and some repeat a year.

Your eyes are shiny with grief and your hands cold. I have seen you cheerful and despairing, with and without masks. Your voice has changed with time, the cries of play mix with the glances of maturity and controlled speech.

You are learning.

I have seen jewels of every kind, real diamonds and fake. The one to decide is the diamond itself, and if I like the less bright one better, I shall take it.

Human beings are made to meet one another; diamonds to be found. You hoe a poor field and find a rich diamond. When it happens, you bury it again straightaway, so that the Mother can mature it a little more.

My earth, rich in stones and rocks!

The earth is a mother full of love, and with love she supports her creatures in the struggle. Struggle and suffering so that they grow, evolve, and change continually.

Evolution through suffering – the need that creates the organ. And then there is the refusal and the fear of suffering by the creatures who will be destroyed by their own fear.

It is immoral that a woman should want to give birth asleep from fear of pain, or rent another's womb to mature her own baby. A child not thought of will be a terrible creature, and the love it did not have will be pain for everyone. The children of pain may inherit the world, if we want them to.

Why avoid an hour's pain, mother, and be anaesthetized at my birth? If you are not there when I arrive, who will be my first mother? Chicks recognize as their mother the first moving thing they see right after birth, be it even a cat, or a tassel moved by the wind. I don't want that.

Mother, if I am deformed it is because they had to pull me out of you with iron tools, like a cyst, a tumor, while you were asleep to avoid the pain.

You were spared an hour's suffering and I have inherited fifty years of pain. You'll see, mother, I shall destroy everyone like you.

You are old now, and of no more use for anything.

I want to help you. So I shall take you, as is so fashionable now, even if you scream, to undergo a little injection at the hospital. I shall kill you, mother, with euthanasia, the good death, so you don't suffer anymore.

Does such a terrible world await us?

Or rather, are we preparing one like that for ourselves?

The children of pain and violence breathe violence and pain.

Most of us avoid pain without ever making the effort to understand it and learn something.[5]

Who knows how to renounce?

Who destroys the world without thinking of our children, who will inherit the destruction?

Shall we show them in books the mythical lion, the fabled tiger, the imaginary anteater? Animals that have disappeared like the dragon and the pterodactyl, the dinosaur and the fox, the eagle and the mythical mermaid?

So is this the way progress and so-called "civilization" expresses itself? They are "civilized," those beings who adapt well to the damaged environment in which they live, and who are bettered by this environment and their own culture?

---

[5] In this new era human beings can once again climb the Mountain of Conciousness. But nothing is to be taken for granted. It is a joyous journey, made of will and responsibility. It is the path of the spiritual warrior, the path of the knight who does not fear the "test" that arises from his own worst aspect, who does not fear pain, who looks "beyond."

Ours is a culture of comic strips, sex films, drugs and profits, violence and gratuitous pain. We torture ourselves and make violence with one another. Where is our civilization?

What traces shall we leave except wounds? I remember ages and customs that disappeared centuries and millennia ago, in the memory of my eternity.

This age is like a tremendous thunderstorm. As the old folks say: "I have never seen the likes of it in all my days."

The wind, indifferent, carves out the black clouds and the ones of smoke. The sea, indifferent, batters its creatures and a fishing boat on the rocks. The earth, indifferent, shakes and knocks down trees and houses.

Has the great clean-up begun? So, has the earth decided to give the floor a good wash and get rid of the excess of ants that are destroying everything? Or will she leave them to annihilate one another?

I know that you are great. I know that your experiences are exceptional, unique, that nobody is as intelligent and capable as you.

Even though you've explored the esoteric, magic and the paranormal for three months, I nod when you say you've already discovered everything ... that the others are incompetent ... that the others are wrong ... that you have immensely great and sublime contacts and already know secrets and powers that no one else has discovered because you are unique. Poor fool!

The mistake of so many is to fall into the web of illusions at the first shot. And then to believe that everything says "yes" only to you. You know nothing!

What, instead, does your death teach you? What shall you learn this time? Have a joyful anxiety to find out, like a child wanting to know what is inside the Easter egg.

Every person contains a hidden and precious surprise. Beyond the image they present of themselves.

Talk to those you dislike instead of avoiding them; you will grow together. But we are lazy, unwilling.

Lord, how many days have I lost in this life of mine? How many days have I spent being truly what I should be? Few I fear. So is my real age a few months instead of 30, 40, or 60 years?

Shall I therefore have to reincarnate many times to make up – a few months for every life – a life fully lived?

And how many lives shall we still need? What utter laziness, and putting it off, and searching for useless pleasures! We are ignorant, immersed in works of art we do not know how to admire and riches we do not want.

And we have the wrong concept of time. If I feel something now, why don't you? And if you feel tomorrow, why don't I too? Courage is being able to reveal our own weaknesses without fear, to show we can cry without being ashamed to do so. Not the courage of fear – which goes from rage to despair – but that of maturity.

The signals coming at me from your eyes, my love, so desperate, so sweet, so vital, so pushy, so delicate, are identical to mine in other moments ... and in the midst is silence. The silence of sighs, of glances over the shoulder, of irritation and incomprehension.

My love, my brother, my companion or true kin of ideas, I am with you.

Even if later, and not now, I am with you.

My body and I are two distinctly different things. I occupy other bodies in other moments, in other distant parts of the world. I think that if I were to meet one of my bodies, at times, I would not be able to recognize it.

At times, I delegate it (my body) some tasks to do, I go away, and when I return it has done them.

However, I stay with it even when it has to carry out unpleasant, tiring jobs, and not just when it is resting.

The grateful and thoughtful kiss of an old lady smacked my cheek. Her trembling embrace closed forcefully around my arms. Her mind, still clear, made her unsteady voice say, "Thank you."

What wisdom and lessons in humility in a few old people! I know that your heart will presumably stop before mine, but if your heart is full of life, it is right. There are still some simple beings who show what direction life should take, who are still worthy of respect and much younger than the young.

I could write of all the sins in the world without repenting mine, for lack of time. And growing old, I should have no more time for counting them than for doing them. Perhaps at this point it is necessary to take a good look at what sins are and separate them into two classes:

First, going against common sense, is a sin against society. In this, I bless the sinners if they are creating with their minds and without excessive violence.

The second is the sin that makes you feel dirty, beyond

customs and common sense, dirty because you know that what you are doing is not right, without hiding from oneself or looking for excuses.

I love you, my love, and our sweet sins harm no one; therefore, if anything, our love is first class!

I have walked in the rain to feel it inside me. I have drunk the rain to purify myself.

I have remembered my divine parts in other places, now. Replying to a brother who was asking about who I was, about my power, I reminded him that to go on a short trip one takes only a small case, and not all of one's baggage.

Every now and then I go and rummage through my things, my "me's" and my memories. No, I don't live on memories, nor do I bask in old successes. On the contrary, I collect in order to once again sow ideas and people.

Who am I? I am. And that is all.

Who have I been? Me.

And you? Us.

I do not wish to be the newborn baby crying and screaming at the world that it is here. I am a laborer of magic. I and me – we are two distinct beings. The I has leapt across centuries and lifetimes and experiences. It is not human. Me, I am here. I live, I feel, I suffer, I struggle, I love, I build a part of my temple. I am an employee of God. I find myself back in another insignificant body which I live in with commitment.

I teach not to be afraid. And not to seek false security (to then be even more afraid). Life is not a barren path, and divine tests are always made of insignificant human doings.

The blow is to be struck where it hurts the most and where we hide our real weakness with false renunciations. "Lord, I am ready to suffer! My arm, oh Lord, tear it from my body! My life, oh Lord!" (But forget that you would make me suffer much more by remembering my jealousy, taking away somebody I love).

The Great Humorist laughs divinely at our weaknesses, our lack of will, the inconsistency of our way of acting that has us going senselessly in and out of the same door like crazy mice. It makes us think we are strong, important, and indispensable; it can do nothing but delude us and suck out our vital lymph.

We are our own parasites. The Divine Force passes through us with its rays, and we do not notice. Become a mirror and you shall reflect God. Do not uselessly waste the energies and the love of Divine Indifference. An indifferent love is not a contradiction; it is rather a means of liberation and evolution from base thoughts eating away at the mind.

I am not speaking of a society like that of Sodom and Gomorrah, but rather of a free Community.

There cannot be free and Universal Love if the lovers are slaves of their passions.

This age binds us to our basest senses more than ever, making us heavy. And all of this creates pain – pain but not purification; rather, suffering, karma, and that is all. If education in this age of transition teaches us malice right from childhood, let us remember that we have been children before, so long ago, even in ages when there was no malice.

And careful, brother: Do not confuse a sensual and purely physical love with sublimated and lasting love.

Whoever you love does not belong to you. The idea of possession is pettiness born of egotism.

How can I love something that is mine? If love is giving and receiving, what can I receive from what is already mine? Unless whomever you think you love is nothing more than a machine to screw. Then that's another matter.

Love is greater than we are. You can love, with passion and emotion and infinite sweetness, but only if you know true Indifference.

Lord, give me the words to make these thoughts understood!

Indifference is not about caring less for others, but rather going through every experience with tranquility and acceptance (not resignation), whether it be sublime or terrifying, pleasant or unpleasant.

The idea of beauty or ugliness, you know, is very relative and limited.

Try to live a new experience without looking for the same old result: "And what about me?"

The ego (more or less my secret; more or less my self-admitted interest) goes away ... if I know Indifference.

God loves with Indifference, remember.

Love with Indifference is creative.

Through Indifference – which one conquers through self-mastery and the type of pain and suffering which liberates and purifies – there is True Love, without possession, without karma, without fears.

To live the moment completely by being oneself, lovers of our beloved love!

If you love with Indifference you truly LOVE. You accept the pain of others upon yourself, you share the earthly karma of a brother and you dilute it with the divine alchemy of Indifference. How can a test weigh upon you if you have True Indifference?

So it is that Indifference is True Love.

Krishna tells Arjuna to kill with Indifference, since he will only be killing bodies already dead, and never the immortal soul.[6]

But be careful not to deceive yourself.

It is not enough to say "I am free," you must be free. Meditate, even with suffering and pain, upon your jealousy, on envy, on the idea of possessiveness, and see to it that the Enemy – seemingly destroyed through meditation – does not return to you transformed, like an old present to which you change only the wrapping paper.

Indifference, for which there is no synonym or translatable word, this esoteric Indifference of which I speak, is composed of: humility (in order to be pure and a brother or sister); dignity (in order to be true, authentic, thought by and precious to God); purity (in one's intent); faith; creative trust; harmony (of behavior and thought); combative aspiration; indomitable commitment; enthusiasm; and obedience. Such Indifference will imprison the selfish beast that is in us – our True Enemy.

True Love means you do not ask recompense for your sacrifice, the sacrifice of your selfish, immature earthly being.

---

[6] With reference to the Hindu epic poem, *Bhagavad Gita*.

"With dignity, oh Lord, I shall not show my wounds," says an ancient, lost song. But what has been lost can be found again.

The downward slope of centuries and millennia can be climbed again with dignity. The time lost by humanity can be regained.

The hidden treasures whose hiding place has been forgotten must be brought back into the Light.

Light! The Resurrection of Humankind!

One day a Master, or rather, the Consciousness inhabiting one of his many bodies, called his own followers to him, who for some time were itching to "go ahead," and he spoke thus:

"You ask me to go beyond the First Door, and you feel full of courage and have faith in your strength; so shall it be. First, however, we shall do a little examination: I shall make real all the fruits of your thoughts, all your thinking, and so we shall see if you truly are brothers and are ready to go forward."

Having said that, he went away in silence. A few days later, the Avatar was ill and feverish. He had wounded a man, stolen, spoken falsely, and sworn. The followers were upset, and he called them to him and said thus:

"I have hit you and robbed you, since your thought has taken form through me. The thoughts you were thinking, the hidden jealousies, your dislikes of one another have done all of this."

Having said this, he continued to love them. And those who were truly ready, even though wounded and robbed, learned Indifference and went beyond the First Shining Door.

I am pain. I who remove it, I hold it close to me like a precious gift. In the small case I have brought along in this life, I have gifts for everyone.

I have Consciousness and I give Consciousness. I give renewal through evolution, which is pain, in the soul as in the body.

It is the function that creates the organ, and the function of an organ that is still missing and not yet formed as it should be, is painful.

So it is for the spirit.

To talk about how great it is to see and about colors, to a blind man is pain. For me as for him.

To show how the leaves light up and become points of light with no flame, torches to the nature spirits, to converse with gnomes, lords of the woods, to joke with naiads and sprites, is Consciousness.

And Consciousness is never loneliness. One is never alone if one knows. But the purification needed to achieve all of this is painful, until it becomes Indifference.

You cannot access the pure esoteric and profound divine magic if you've been raised in a pen and have never scratched around and struggled, if you have not fed on earth and stones.

Blind man, you cannot see because you keep your eyes closed! Open them and you shall see!

But first, may you receive a beating. May pain purify you from the sin of wanting but not knowing how to open your eyes! I have thrown my log on your human fire. I have sat among you and talked to you. But I have also listened and absolved, I have taken on myself a few burdens still too heavy for you.

May knowing pain prepare you, if thus it is right.[7]

Make of me what your Consciousness suggests.

If you prefer to insult me, I am ready. Sometimes, too often, the destruction of the symbol has been essential to free Consciousness from the body, because men were immature.

Christ with the cross has become *the* symbol of pain!

Horus was cut into pieces and they were thrown into the delta of the Nile. And so again for so many ... many other times ... but for a few exceptions.

The human and the Divine in each of us are confused and intertwined, and it is not easy to distinguish them. Faith is lacking, and we fear deceit because Indifference is a long way off.

Someone asked me what form some nature spirits had: In one book they appeared as beautiful, tall blond youths; in another, the same were gelatinous and shapeless. What a divine, humorous difference!

But all the nature beings appear to us, as we with our thought want to see them! Thought is a powerful creator, and if it already works on the physical forces by means of our hands, think what power it develops on much subtler, delicate, moldable energies like those which give a "body" to the nature spirits! And as we give form to these beings, without ever possessing them, they give energies to us.

---

[7] The esoteric journey need not be one of suffering. It is true, however, that most people learn through suffering. Although inevitable, pain may be an opportunity for understanding, for growth, and evolution. "Healing," in this case, means welcoming that which synchronic events bring and eventually learning from them.

They mould us as we mould them; they see us as they wish to see us, through their and our power of Maya.

It is our thought, our thought forms that confuse us and envelop us, through the force of each person, and stir the human with the Divine. It is we who distance faith and call up deceit, because we do not make our Indifference mature.

In the wood I greeted one of the Lords of the place, the gnome of an old oak, and he, taking possession of a caterpillar, wrote his name on the earth, by making it crawl. The grass bent down, and the being, creating a cushion for me, invited me to sit and talk to him.

Out of good manners, knowing the etiquette, I accepted the stem of wild sorrel to suck on, which the Lord of the place pointed out to me. Then we talked at length.

This is reality, only normally you are not aware of it. How many times in a wood, will a gnome tug in vain at your trousers to get you to stop and talk to him! And you, too thick in your incredulous body, do not stop. The blind man, who does not see, believes in the light he is told about!

Talk to the trees, and a thundering voice will speak back to you from the chestnut tree, and a frail one from the willow, a sweet one from the cherry tree, a firm and wise one from the walnut tree! Children, who have happily learned this, say "sorry" quite naturally when they bump into a branch.

A very small girl told me that, at times, she gets nervous and a little afraid when she talks to me. This grieves me, but it often happens, rarely with children, more often with adults. Can it be because, for many, I represent the Father figure a little?

Two natures compete and contrast within me: the physical one limited to the present incarnation, and the much more ancient one, which is Consciousness.

There is a battle inside: between the powers and the desire (and, at times, the need to use them); the maturity that remembers: "Much power to he who does not use it"; the apparent megalomania and the inner yearning for simplicity; the memories of the present life and infinite ones from past and contemporaneous lives; between a sanguine, instinctive, emotional personality and a self-control that hardly lets anything show.

After all, it is the artistic emotion of riding a wild colt with an expert soul. Why do I say artistic? Because being able to stay in the saddle is a matter of style, of refinement, of dexterity ... and it is so difficult!

This body so weak, that gets tired and wears itself out, that exalts itself, struggles with itself, humiliates itself, wounds itself – so unsuited to the spirit, so dull and heavy. It is like the rough marble that the artist will manage to sculpt with blows of chisel and will.

Our soul is the artist who struggles against the veins and cracks of passions, who skillfully and with pain knows how to bring out of the marble the pure figure that has been forever imprisoned within.

And despair is our enemy. When I am weak and lost and sad and insecure, when I feel the seasons and the winters and the summers go racing through me, and when I have the impression that they are too fast for me and that there is not enough time to do what is written, I turn my head to the heavens and ask for explanations: Is it not perhaps written that all that is necessary will be accomplished?

Even if I see the work pile up and the carriages of our train slow down, don't I know that the rail tracks are already drawn and universal Divine Consciousness is waiting for us at the station?

God, what are you waiting for? Has your providence ever left me alone? Of course not, even if my physical body complains and unfairly considers your company not enough (how could it ever be?). I know that every time I asked, you never refused me anything, if it was right.

Human loneliness and isolation are the humorous consequence of the exercise of Consciousness (which is universal). I am so much with and within everybody that I seem to be alone!

I live in the Consciousness and the Unconsciousness of every creature: I am fly, and horse, and falcon, and fish in the sea, and grass on the hill. Oh, if only Humankind could see how it tortures itself thinking it is torturing other species!

I am the rabbit in the breeding farm, and the calf shut suffocating in a truck, and the tuna and the dolphin hacked to death, I am the tree sawn down to its roots, and the dog abandoned on the street by its owner, desperate and without love. I am, we are, you are the poisoned apple, the sea gull who drowns in the oil slick, the animal vivisected with a sneer of delight, and the slave, and the exploited, the suicide, the lover, and the madman.

Your pain is deeply mine, as much as Consciousness is condemnation and disgust for what we choose – when it is evil and pain, or divine exaltation, when it is goodness and love.

Love, love – a word used with a thousand meanings and a thousand falsehoods, but also with a thousand-and-one purities, ritual sacredness, and elevations of the soul.

Universal Consciousness, deep down inside the race minds, is Universal Love.

Knowledge is the purpose of Humankind and of life. Knowledge of everything, the vision of every reality through millions of facets of the crystal, the only one called Truth. Truth, which has a thousand names, opposing and seemingly contrary Truths, because your vision is limited and not universal.

And yet it is so easy to enter into Consciousness!

But if you do not possess Indifference you will not succeed, because you would be destroyed by it. To open up your mind into a universal breath with the rhythm of the world. To be tree and leaf and cloud and mountain. To be the buttercup coming out of the earth after being a dead, buried seed, and now reborn much lovelier! To be a letter rich in words and, therefore, a thinking creature!

Truth – I used to write on my closet of secrets – is BEING! Truth is Being! All that Is! All that you think has a correspondence in the REAL!

Maya, power of Maya, is to create what is thought, then everything that you think of is created. We maintain ourselves conscious of Creation by creating. We fashion ourselves in billions of times, actions, events, and places.

The quasi-real, which is the only reality in that it is subjective, is transformed into Universal Consciousness, which is objective reality. Thus the egg is born from the egg, and the tree from itself, and the stone shoots forth crystals, and the light its own shadow.

Creation follows all the directions, explodes in spirals toward the inner and the outer. Time is a road to travel freely. God, the immovable mover, thinks himself and everything contains, without being contained.

The Book of the Universe is kept on the knees of the Great Observer or Great Book-Keeper, who marks down for caterpillar as for man, for alien and different beings, for unimaginable species, every result of their thoughts and their actions.[8]

Alongside the astonishing feats of a general, he marks down how much cheese the poor mouse has stolen, how many petals the cicada has nibbled, how many Holy Avatars have changed their worlds, how many bubbles the fish has blown to create its airy refuge – one alongside the other, he records, with sublime Indifference.

Because if the mouse is given to nibbling, this is its nature and its duty has to be done, in the same way, if a Master is given to teaching, that is not merit, but his nature.

---

[8] The "Great Bookkeeper," in the ultimate analysis, is our inner self. It is the truest, most Divine part of us, free from self-justification, which after death judges and directs itself through continuous experience.

How many coins have you been given, brother? One or one hundred?

And you, what can you do with your talents? Don't be shy. You are always given more talents than you think. Take a good look at the bottom of your bag: The gold coins, the heaviest ones, are at the bottom! Spend the silver ones to prepare a good investment for your gold. Believe in yourself. Wash away laziness, anxiety, and fear.

You can go forth with courage even into the storm, if you know that that light down the valley is your home.

Do not waste this life!

If work, as they say, ennobles you, try to make a few distinctions: Whether your satisfaction in work comes from cleaning the stairs, or clipping dogs, or compiling useless columns of figures, give all of yourself to your work and offer it, but do not limit yourself to the work that brings in the bread.

Do not be a slave of the useless. Any work ennobles if you do it nobly and with dignity. Working for what is superfluous makes you a slave of the useless. Grow inside by living the moment, build the world that belongs to you with your mind and your imagination.

As Pythagoras says, "Don't sit on top of a heap," which means: Do not do useless things.

At times, the despair of having lived uselessly takes away our courage to continue and go on. At times, from an apparently objective analysis of ourselves, it seems we are here, useless and aimless in life. At times this happens to those who SEEK.

Remember, when you are not yet ready and you presumptuously try to seek yourself and presumptuously decide you are worthless, remember that this may be one of the tests to overcome. The Lords of Karma decide for you at times, and they test you to the limit, and just as the sword is to be beaten, heated, and cast into the water to be tempered, so it is with your Consciousness.

If you find closed doors, it may be because your key is not yet ready. Seek with courage and you will find it in your hand.

Do not think only of yourself, but of others first, and you will be first. Fight for a thought and no fear or dread will touch you. Go beyond your strength and you will find yourself invincible and invulnerable.

You will have the strength of Indifference. A man who believes is worth thousands of men who cannot believe.

I have said that God is the Eternally Indifferent, and I should like to explain why: God is Infinite Consciousness, is all creatures. How can he take sides with some of them, if all of them are him?

Just as the *Bhagavad Gita* says, God is in all creatures but they are not in him.

And God thinks of himself through the Creation. God thinks of himself through his own creatures. And every creature attains Knowledge of all Creation, through the search for it from their own point of view.

The ant experiences evolution by increasing its knowledge of its own world through pain, which is evolution. The tree, which has senses very different from our human ones, knows the other creatures in its own way. As Consciousness, I am tree, ant, man and every creature is in me.

There is always an awakened Consciousness for every cycle of existence and, as the Chinese say, Buddha is always and continuously incarnated. Buddha is, naturally, like Christ, a Consciousness.

Evolution is the result of God's continuous thinking of himself. The changing of a creature's body and mind is evolution, whether it be in the acquisition of greater Knowledge or in the creation and specialization of a new organ.

Whereas God is infinite and contemporaneous Consciousness, a minor divinity is Consciousness limited in time and space, an organ of the ultimate God.

Then there is the eternally present Consciousness limited to the creatures. It is us. We as in "royal plural," I mean. This Consciousness helps the different creatures in the pursuit of Knowledge, which is the GOAL of all creatures. When all the Knowledge is found, it becomes Consciousness, conscious Consciousness.

I love you, creatures all. And I offer my arm to the mosquito, so that I, the mosquito, may feed on me. I am the warm rock on which I rest. And the two ants fighting between themselves. How can I favor the black one or the red one, if both are me? This is the Indifference in swatting my I-fly, because I see and take part in the two modes of being. But often I prefer to fly away, rather than be swatted by myself.

The insect on my finger is me. I watch through faceted eyes what my human Consciousness is producing on this paper. And with my insect psychology I laugh and do not understand my waste of words.

Oh human Consciousness, I have lit a ritual fire to read inside your "I," to determine if you are telling and thinking the Truth, brother.

I listen to you as you speak, and I stare, I-Us, at the fire. I know you also like this, being you. The harmony of I-Us makes these things happen.

The importance of the ritual is its infinite power beyond time. The ritual, indeed, is always One.

And from life to life, from action to action, the same work is continued. The ritual is a work of art to which you add new strokes of color. My brothers, if the path is designed to be travelled together, the rite to be celebrated together, make sure that your Consciousness has appropriate thought forms. Otherwise, it will be a picture of black and grey, and a ritual of little value. If each one of you is an essential color for the work, make sure that the expected color is there, always.

And the sunflowers have bowed their heads, the clouds have gathered, and the shooting stars have written the names of God in the heavens with their dust. And the rhythms of life and the spirals of existence have opened and closed.

And the symphonies of the grass, and the plants, and the voices of all the creatures have come forth from all throats.

And every plant has offered up the fruits of its own existence. And the light has emitted all its rays. Evolution and action is the prayer of all creatures.

You may pray with fine words and fine actions, or even just with words and actions.

Your art is your existence. Every life is one more brick to build your temple. Yours, Consciousness, minor God, infinite God of the Gods.

The moon has found its way again, and the seasons their course. The wanderer his path, and ignorance its light. Everything, again and again, has been said, and done, and thought.

Love has been loved, time blessed, and God thanked.

Let us learn to laugh with the Humorist and not make him laugh at us and our pettiness. And may the grass continue to grow and the flowers to be thought beautiful. And may Intelligent Harmony continue to revolve the spirals of being.

Being that is Truth.
Truth that is Being.

The Master is tired. He has talked for long hours into the night, as it grew darker and darker while the fire grew brighter and brighter.

He has replied to a thousand questions and has given rise to as many in the minds of the men, women, and children who were listening to him.

His voice, warm and calm, gentle and steady; his gestures, tender and strong; his face, colored by the fire – express all his power.

Now he will rest. And tomorrow evening, after working the earth, he will start again to awaken their Consciousness.

His figure, despite being so warm, unfortunately incites awe in those around him. Is he therefore condemned to remain alone?

Here we are, once again, with those who gather round the fire to listen to him in the evening.

PART THREE

Solitude of Consciousness which yet penetrates a thousand creatures! Illusion and credulity of existences and of whys and wherefores.

Apparent and deceiving Truth outside being.

We are shut in the box of our own reality, and Consciousness comes to blow the lid off!

The *Qabalah* gives us the measurements of God, for whom we shall make a nice suit with our little boxes of fake indifference and pettiness.

Are we worthy to be worn by him?

How many people ask me how I am? And if I am happy with my choices? Has this thought crossed their minds?

Things that change are always seen subjectively, it is true. And the good father worries, not for himself, but for how his innocent children will react to his choices or will be affected by them. He talks with each one of them and listens to their problems. All big ones. Or about how they see, judge, and consider the personal situations of their father.

Traumatized, weak, insecure, their feelings hurt. Who of them remembers, in their own egotism, that even their father may need help?

How many have passed the test and have not thought solely of themselves and of how they can egotistically see, accept, judge? How many times have I repeated: "Think of others."

There was once a king who lived with his court and his ministers, and he took care of governing the kingdom with them. The kingdom prospered in spite of court feuds and the threats from other governments.

One day the king, who administered justice with indifferent love and shared the wealth among the people, chose for himself a woman with whom he wanted to live. The court, and those who feared losing the favors of the king, rose up and protested: The king really should not have done this to them! And the tongues tried to bite, and the jealousies of the ministers swelled up. Only a small, humble peasant woman at the market said: "Everybody is concerned with what they are losing or gaining and nobody thinks about love. I haven't heard a minister say, 'What does the bride feel? Do they love each other?' Nobody cares at all. And yet the laws say that our kingdom is based upon love! What will the king do now?"

Even if at times I feel discouraged, brothers, I love you precisely because you are egotists, small and weak, because you ask without giving, because you do not understand and you puff up with presumption, because you are extremists in your thoughts, because you are too timid, because you underestimate yourselves and, therefore, act like fools without being so, because not one of you wants to give up something to be with the others, because you think everything is owed to you ...

I am with you, brother, but have you renewed yourself?

What does it mean to renew oneself, if not becoming a little more the others and less our egotistical self?

I love you because you always have the secret idea of being right and that the others see you wrongly, and because at times, too often, you spit out judgments while, in reality, you are the accused ones.

Thundering, God reminded us that he does not need Humankind, but Humankind needs him, just as the ant needs crumbs, and the fish water, and the creatures of the earth air.

See to it, brothers and sisters, that a ritual is always lived fully, with all your bodies united FOR THE OTHERS. That the words of prayer are not empty sounds, spoken just to open your mouths and air your tongues.

Let yourself go, brother. If you talk to the trees you cannot be selfish. If you build castles in the air, do not waste this splendid work. Let yourself live with indifferent emotion and build the foundations of your castle: It will be more real than ever!

Have the taste of struggle in your mouth, but for great things, not petty ones. It is the little things that create the great disputes. One is always in agreement on the important things.

Be hunters – hunters of yourselves.

To live together means to give, not to expect.

Looking into people's hearts is a hard task. Beneath the thin layer of good upbringing there is the filth and slime of egotism.

Now I am also a road-sweeper of the esoteric or, rather, a skier, because I can slide without falling on the rubbish, as if it were pure snow.

At times, the last are truly the first, but knowing it must not make them proud. Are the greatest thus the weakest, hence to be helped for a longer time?

The flier navigates with surety in a twilight world, where the shadows are not illusions, where what seems is, where what appears sure is fluttering fog. His line of flight is straight and cuts through the mountains of thought and the valleys of Consciousness.

Do not nurse your putrid corpse, composed of passions and unruly instincts. How can you live if your parts do not obey you? If your heart beats every now and then, and the lungs breathe by chance, and your blood does not respect the path of its veins?

What are the important things in life? The profits for old age that will not be there, or the now breathed into the woods after the rain? A solid affection promised to last the duration of the matrimonial contract, or the intense, unforgettable moment of the now? Which might last longer?

The complete, superior human being is never alone, even in the middle of the desert or far from the hearts of his kind.

My great love, it is not foolish that I love you in silence. I have your image inside me and I look at you in secret. It does not matter if you know nothing of me; you are all women, all the femininity of the Creation – even if you do not know it. You are the other face of the sun, and of God. You are the universal balance of Creation. And as opposites attract, so inevitably we are drawn together.

Our subtle bodies are joined and you do not know it.

The most important parts of our being belong to each other in indifferent and passionate love.

What does it matter if our physical illusions still do not know each other? I have been caressing your soul forever, and you do not know my name.

We have made love joining our ethereal bodies, and my negligible physical body has not even held your hand. Who are you? I am you! I have been married according to forgotten rites. I have loved with passion and forgotten and remembered. I have found after a thousand years the person I could not have kept away from me for more than a day without going crazy.

The divine chessboard hosts one, single, immense game. God plays chess with himself and always wins.

To lose, and to find again, what sense does it make? What can you lose in eternity that contains everything?

So the tear returns to the eye that cried it and the leaf to the tree it fell from. And the earth to the sun that generated it and the voice to the mouth that emitted it. The crumbs re-form the bread and you, my love, return to me.

The ever-open spiral of time rejoins upon brief lines every existence and every thought.

The divine breath, which is word, creates solid thoughts and weavings of conscious existences.

Like everything we *seem* to be living.

Why all this fear of death? Death as a dream, within divine illusion.

The dream descended from On High and slipped upon me. Life has taken on new unthought-of meanings, and the vibration of the world and of all the creatures – ten cycles per second – has pulsed through my every fiber. I make this pulsation conscious, and I am in the mind of every creature.

The bright mind of crystals and the dark intelligence of the mud of the abysses are one thing. The strong leafy thought of the fir trees and the quivering, trembling mind of the moss are chords of the same instrument. The flashing thought of the frisky dolphins is embroidered on the heavy warp of the human mind.

Thus every being is part of more complex Consciousnesses. Cells with personal problems make up a liver, which is but an organ of a more complicated being, and this being takes part in the life of the race, and the whole race makes up vaster and Divine Beings.

Is man the God of his own forefinger? Can the finger do without its own God? Do the cells of the fingertip have an awareness of being part of a vaster life?

Life is not to be confused with form. Form is not significant. The goal of beings is to take part in the existence of ever more complex entities.

Humankind is not at the high point of earthly life, but is placed midway, exactly at the point of equilibrium on the Great Scales that weigh the material and the spiritual.

Humankind is a point of passage, a stage on the journey that all life undertakes. Race mind, minor Divinities, the spiritual arm of the scales of life is a thousand million times longer than the physical one.

What is the weight of a dream? And that of a thought of love? How many meters or kilometers long is the I in my mind?

Every Consciousness of me is multiplied by the being of which I am part.

And a foot is no less important than the heart, and the sphincter counts no less than the brain. How could I think without an anus? I would not be a whole being and I would not have physical life. What would I do without lungs or without a heart? Each of our parts is no less noble than the others, just as each of our places in the world is no less essential than any other.

The stupidity of pride in one's own social status demonstrates the miserable pettiness of whoever feels they are great. Honor to the base, not the top!

Who is more a servant than a brain which must take care of all?

Love and Indifference, spiritual elevation means doing one's duty well.

Duty is ritual.

As Consciousness, I have no presumption of being a flea or a man, a stunted plant or a sleek tiger. I am.

I am what my servant decides for me, I participate intensely, I live only the moment in which I, Consciousness, am always someone else.

Since I participate in everything and I am everything, I have the immortality of vital transition.

I do not fear what does not exist: death. I learn and I obtain Knowledge in the mutable transformation of death. I love the transformation and the multiform voluptuousness of the species.

I am the bacteria in the air you are breathing, brother, and I come into your lungs. Now, I am a drop of your blood, rich with oxygen, and I go up through your veins to your brain.

Now I am you.

I am what I touch, my I brother, You-Me. This is communion.

I participate without acting, now, but I could do so. Even in writing.

I can pinch your nose with your own right hand or play with your heart. Can you feel it beating? Beating and pulsating? Feel the blood flowing into your temples, warm. This is you: a sack full of sea water walking around.

Do you know that the composition of blood is almost identical to that of seawater? The sea is us.

Our body. Our diving suit. The garment we wear. Form.

We take birth and we float for nine months in a sack full of water, the amniotic fluid. When the dressmaker, our mother, has finished the garment, we put it on.

New bodies, new thoughts. Every time that, as Consciousness, I participate in the existence of a creature, it is like dying and being reborn. There is the darkness of Consciousness, full of the freedom of every imaginable frequency, painful and exalting, a point of very dense emptiness, and the awareness of the sole rhythm of the world, so constant and eternal: ten jolts per second.

In the pause, eternal, between one beat and another I open new eyes (if they are eyes), within a new body. And I think and I perceive with new images of existence and new problems.

I am the patient spider upon the web, and I pray to God for my daily fly (no more than the shopkeeper, awaiting his client in his nook). I am the caterpillar on the cabbage leaf, happy, and the bird that devours the caterpillar, and the falcon that beats down on the crow, and the heinous hunter that kills the falcon for pleasure. I am, and I feel, thoughts and feelings. But I do not participate except when my mission requires it.

But why do I tell you these things? So that you can be Consciousness with me.

To know, to believe, so as to BECOME.

To know, to get to know, so as to BE.

To get to know new Truths, new changeable faces on the great crystal of the Ultimate Truth.

To seek, creatively, means to attain Knowledge.

To get to know the Truth, to know the Being, the Truth that is Being.

The Truth is relative to whoever knows it, to the life (aware presence) that subjectively seeks Knowledge.

And that which lives in a bacterium, in its life of thirty seconds, is as dense as what the mayfly, flying around, learns and lives in twelve hours, or what the ant consigns to memory and experience in three years, and a dog in sixteen, and a man in seventy.

And a human being – the pivot of the Great Scales – can be the aware presence and Consciousness, and live an intense life in thirty seconds or twelve hours.

An explosion of awareness makes the birth and death of a fetus as intense and valid as an incarnation of thirty years.

I shall speak further of the marvels of Consciousness, and of the infinite web that binds every Consciousness to the other selves, to the other individual awarenesses of this and other worlds.

And this one is already so vast, oh Lanoo,[9] that the writing would already be infinite in describing it and in showing you the multiform essences of life.

A houseplant, for example: It is not the leaves and the stems that you see, for these are merely the denser part of it, like the skeleton in a man. Some beings perceive us

[9] Lanoo is a level of initiation at Damanhur's School of Meditation.

only as skeletons, and they do not see the internal organs or the skin.

So it is for us with trees: We see only their denser parts. Others see us in the form of a pulsating, colored egg. Others still cannot manage to perceive us except as something very fast, a lightning bolt passing by, randomly restless. A phenomenon of nature ...

And for you, human being, could not a lightning bolt be alive? Or a being made solely of sounds, like the thunder?

When, oh Lanoo, you approach the trunk of a tree to talk to it, you are already inside the tree three steps away. And why, deliberately deaf and blind, do you not see the gnomes, the fairies, the beings that, conscious of you, pass through you and tickle you?

There are creatures that play at sliding on the rays of your sight, or put ribbons on your thoughts, knotting them, dense as shoelaces. Some beings play on the swings of your gold earrings, or swim in your rings, and immerse themselves in the chain you wear around your neck; this metal is perfumed for them and its emanations are delicious.

You see it is not poetry, but the wonderful divine reality to which we belong. Our most hidden and secret thoughts are shining like neon signs in the night a few meters above our heads. The feelings we would most wish to hide out of modesty are sung in chorus like national anthems by dozens of creatures perched on our shoulders or lying down on our hair ...

The Great Humorist, in our minds, looks like a fat and cheerful Father Christmas, or an isosceles triangle, or a rolling cloud, or a spider's web that envelops and permeates the universe ... and every image is real. The laughter of God is that vibration of ten cycles that keeps life alive and one.

A thought nourishes many beings, and a castle in the air gives hospitality to many forms.

A thought of hatred is a bomb or an earthquake that kills many creatures.

Continually living in the past, in memories, in regret, in the subtle pain of masochistic self-analysis, is a volcano that pours molten lava over many, many innocent creatures.

Just as when, for us, a volcano is in eruption, it is the earth that is crying and pouring hot, destructive tears. And the earthquakes are sobs of pain, and the tornadoes and the cyclones, sighs of regret.

Life is One, and for this reason every form (species) depends on others.

We are in symbiosis with the little beings (cells) that make up our body, with the beings (vegetables-animals) on which we feed, with the creatures that feed on us and our thoughts, and so on ... with the Divinity that presides over our race, and the God of the Gods.

My love, what we feel for each other is the rain that gives life to the scorched fields of thousands upon thousands of creatures; it is the grain that sways heavily, rustling and ready for an abundant harvest; it is sweet smelling bread just out of the oven. Let us nourish one another and the universe with love, my love.

Your image is great and gentle and scented. Indeed my being loves love, not the object of it. I love the completion, the fulfillment, the femininity that is the missing match in you to my masculinity.

You know that your name and your face do not count; so many and musical are your mutable sweet names, oh my source.

Solitude weighs so heavy because it does not produce reciprocal love, and it is like clouds of dust and not of rain, ears of wheat standing straight and without seeds, grand beautiful houses, but not lived in.

But when the water becomes cloud and children live in the houses, everything is completed.

And all are happy, nourished by our love.

I caress your image sitting on my knees with your head resting on my shoulder; I can feel your warm breath on my neck and the fire of your love enveloping me.

It is thus that the irreconcilable meet: water and fire, hot and cold, light and dark.

From the union of opposites a new universe springs forth.

My love pulsates on the rhythm of your love, and your image with your beautiful and unknown face becomes more dense and alive.

What we feel for each other is music, and fine foods, and spiraling waves of pure happiness that flow flashing through the universe.

In the chest of our hearts are stored all the treasures that unite us in the past and in the present. Sweet memories, objects impregnated by our auras joined in shared, exalted, or foolish experiences. But important to us, like the secret games preserved by children. Now, little things of ours bring back thoughts and feelings in communion.

This immense wealth is the granary of all the creatures in tune with us.

Holding hands, my love, gives off sparks that light up our little friends' woodland cities for years. The forms of fairies, gnomes, undines envelop us in happy dances, walking on the light air around us as on a spiral staircase.

Smiling, they pop their heads up out of the earth and disappear among the leaves of the trees, letting their feet dangle for a moment. They say that the leaves rustle not because of the wind, but because of their dance steps.

If you love me, your eyes will see, my love, the gifts they leave, curtseying, at our feet: arabesqued leaves, a bundle of music, a bracelet of scent, a tiara of smiles, a necklace of kisses. It is what they can offer us – their most precious things – in exchange for the nourishing song of our love.

And these things are essential for us too. Our auras are joined thanks to their work, our thought has us live the moment more intensely thanks to their activity.

And all this is fuel for our evolution.

My love, I have not spoken of your age; as the proverbs know, love does not grow old. We may have one day of love, or meet again after a thousand years. We are our image, and your hands caressing me are forever young and delicate.

If our bodies are old, what does it matter? Cannot two young tramps love one another? If my clothes are crumpled and your skirt patched, can this stop the pulsating of our blood?

How beautiful is youth which flees nonetheless.
Of the morrow there's no certainty.
Whoever wants to be happy, so may they be ...

Let us live now, not tomorrow. Let us love now. The spring of our love will never know winter, because now it is spring.

I have seen some old people hold hands with tenderness and walk, happy and limping, at each other's side. This is the serene image of love.

I would like, my love, for you and I to be old, and grey, and limping. I would like for your hands to have the rare tenderness of an eighty-year-old. Never an age of decline, but a continual culmination of the shared bond of a thousand experiences lived together.

I would like a mature love, made of trust and secret sweetness, where the things done for whom one loves are not declared to have some merit, but are palpitating and tender secrets.

Everything is already known to our thought-of thoughts, sung before the spectators of the subtle world.

I would like a very young, adolescent love, full of madness and emotion.

I want you, my love, who are all these things – whatever your name and your secret names are.

I have seen two rays of colored light make a knot, while, together, we were passing under the rainbow. They invited us to the celebrations that are always held around the pot of gold in the evening, at the end of every rainbow.

They were all there with us. The moon, the night, the warm air, the crickets of the fields, our hands intertwined. Our dream has once again nourished the spirits of the earth; all the species come out reinvigorated. And what if we too were a dream of theirs?

What if *everything* were a dream of God?

A legend says that God fell asleep, and we are his dreams. Wake up, God!

And give me an answer, just a little one that we can understand to know who we really are.

Everything is Maya, illusion. With the fire of thought we forge the iron of our existence.

Lucifer was a dream that rebelled against his dreamer, and dreamed for himself. Like Prometheus, he brought humanity the Light of Knowledge, the freedom to make mistakes.

And God dreamed it all, amused. Perhaps, it is a strange way of dreaming, even though what has no comparisons cannot be strange. The dreams dreamed, dream in their turn, and act in the dream at their discretion. Is this free will?

And are they our dreams, so dense, that become free creatures?

Dying to learn.

But death, in this incarnation, represents RENEWAL.

Have you renewed yourself, brother? Did you die last night and are you reborn this morning?

Do you understand the high significance of being free? Free from ourselves? To be free means being able to obey.

Your hand can do anything at all: write, hoe, sculpt, and paint. It is therefore free and, if it is not presumptuous, free to obey the brain.

So many fear for their freedom. The best realize that, in proceeding to climb the tree of initiation, only their apparent freedom is eliminated, while the authentic freedom of Knowledge opens up. The power of their own freedom.

Much power to those who do not use it, also means much freedom to those who are able to obey. The idea of "freedom" is born of egotism. You already know what I mean.

Is the worker free to get up at five o'clock in the morning to go to the factory? And to relax only on Sundays? Or to be a chicken in a cage, crushed, tied down, the perfect slave, not even aware of being a slave?

I preach FREEDOM!

Freedom given by Knowledge, by Consciousness, by Evolution.

Free yourself by obeying. Free yourself in Indifference. Free yourself in faith and in research, aiming at the goal, at the final purpose. Free yourself through initiation. And what does initiation mean, if not liberation?

But when selfishness makes us blind, when the illusion of our ego and the refusal to renounce things dazzle us, we are afraid of losing our freedom ... without even knowing what it is.

Initiation teaches you self-sufficiency; it gives you Consciousness of being; it breaks the ties with things that are overly superfluous.

The illusion of being free to be able to smoke! Or drink! Or eat to excess to the point of waste!

And what a curse is this last thing! Plenty is not eating three courses one after the other and overloading the body. Are you free when you must eat a lot because you think you feel more secure this way?

Or when you must sleep a lot because you believe you recover from your tiredness in this way? Or smoke because you can't do without it? Are you free to be a slave to pleasures that are obligations and dependencies and slavery?

You are free to smoke, drink, sleep, eat ... and refuse Knowledge.

Free will is the possibility of making mistakes, but also of attaining Knowledge. Even drawing close to God. Of reaching the immense power of REALIZATION!

When you understand and truly realize yourself for others and not for yourself, when you eat little so that others have more food, when you work with commitment so that others benefit from your work, when your effort is prayer and continual offering – don't look at all the costs for the job you like. Obey in your work and you will be free.

Or else refuse all of this.

Don't want the thorns, the harsh path, the effort? Enjoy your illusion and call us stupid, if this gives you strength and is something you can't do without, like the cigarette you hold between your lips or the fork you hold in your hand.

Individuality is splendid if it is not transformed into a selfish search for self-affirmation.

Once there was a train; rather, there is and there always will be. It was made up only of uncomfortable carriages, freezing cold in winter and boiling in summer. But so many of us being together, all in all, made the journey bearable. But not for everyone.

Some decided to get off the train and continue by car. So they got off at the very next station, said good-bye, and carried on, soon overtaking the slow train. Travelling alone, or in twos or threes, was much more comfortable.

With intelligence, and adjusting well to the driving, the travelers sped swiftly on their way, and with a pinch of pride smiled and said: "See, we had the courage to get off and free ourselves, and now we are proceeding much faster!"

The tarmac mountain road led them up to a large square with a splendid panoramic view. Then the road ended. There were high impassable mountains on one side and ravines on the other.

The motorists did not know what to do, and waited. Some time later the train came puffing by, and so as not to lose speed, could not stop for the occupants of the car. Thus, it disappeared into the mountain tunnel, suited only to the passage of the small train.

From the high plain, the motorists, having got out of their vehicle, saw the slow train gradually disappear into the wonderful blue valley beyond the mountains, towards its goal.

Fire, I listen to your voice.

You know my story and part of my secrets.

Tell. We have known one another forever: Your flames have obeyed me; they have written for me in time and space.

The fire of the stars in the icy universe – that, after all, is not as cold as they say – has sighed many times with my name ... or that of the one to whom I belong, which is whoever.

Not even this time shall I have a life of rest.

I feel myself called upon once again. And even, at times, a little bored of doing the same things, of repeating the same things, of showing the same things, of having the same faces in front of me, of hearing the same questions and perceiving the same fears – when it is so easy to free myself!

Faith, my children, faith! Devotion, love, commitment ... but that's already too many things.

Wanting to have faith, at least. *Wanting* to reach the goal. At least realizing that a life lived any other way is wasted.

Lord, millions of men and women have prayed before fire for thousands of years. The formulas thought of and their methods have made solid and powerful rituals.

Lord, grant once more that my open arms before the sacred fire reach out and rise up without fear. Grant that my arms hold – in a single embrace – all the weak, presumptuous, timid children of mine. They are but the projection of my weak, presumptuous, and timid human image. Grant that their eyes might see a moment of your Truth.

Make them united, strong, aware and courageous.

Continue to make the Spirit of Knowledge descend upon them, even if they are not yet aware of it. I care so much about them, you know!

Make them sincere, Lord, sincere in their intents. Remind them that this is not a human game, but rather a divine test of their maturity!

Lord, make them presumptuous and courageous in you, not timid. It will not be presumption but real strength in themselves through Consciousness.

Make them strong in you, not weak. Enlighten them and grant that they begin to UNDERSTAND!

To comprehend the wonderful goal awaiting them, the glory and the nobility of their being HERE!

They must hear your voice within: through faith when there is not yet comprehension. With devotion when there is not yet Consciousness.

ATTENTION

Take everything from the best, Lord. Grant that they feel despair, that they feel alone and betrayed. Grant that their naivety and purity be thwarted and put to the test.

If they will accept this. Remember that, from whoever is really on the path of purity, nothing can be taken, because nothing belongs to them.

How many wounded "me's"! How much weakness and pretence at not understanding!

You, who are new on the path, you cannot not understand! Within you are all the answers and all the Truths. You just have to be able to read them! To *feel* what is true!

Do not think only of pleasure or making up for lost pleasure, or new pleasure. Do not feel stupid if "you too" do not have the things that others have.

If you think you do not have love, remember it is yours, that of everyone!

Sublimation!

Remember that you lose nothing!

That you are not "any less" and that you are not alone!
I love those who are alone more, because they are closer
to me.

Because they are closer to everyone!

And control your temper! Not long faces, but smiles of
joy! Not fixed ideas about who is good or bad, about who
you think is doing something to you or who is not!

Think about what you do for others, not what others
can do, or not do, for you! Give, don't take! Give without
looking or judging what others do for you. Make a vow
of giving yourself completely! You will be raped, trampled
underfoot, used like an object, they will have you go round
and round like a donkey attached to a grindstone, and
your body little by little will be refined!

But without FAITH, all this is impossible.

Fashion yourselves in obedience. Obliterate yourselves
in the execution of your work and your thought!

Commit esoteric suicide for the others who do not
respect you, who do not love you, who do not notice you,
who do not consider you, who do not see you, who scorn
you, whom you can't stand! I am with you, brother.

Have you renewed yourself?

Even if I don't speak to you, I smile when you are not
looking at me, and I say inside myself: "Good ... go on. Like
that a bit more and you're there. Come on ... strength and
courage!"

But I pretend not to notice you, I don't encourage you.
If anything, I chide and criticize you. Yet, you feel that I am
with you, that I don't take my eyes off you even for a second.

I know, Lanoo, Elder Brother and Sister, what is going on in your hearts and your minds.[10] I know your sins, your thoughts, your outbursts, even the things you try to hide from yourself ... because I am you. Universal Consciousness isn't only a word.

I want everything from you. I expect for you to grow, to suffer. I want the fire of renewal to devour you.

I want to kill you, torture you, destroy the evil that is in you. If you so want. If you ask me.

Remember that your evil is mine. That you are me.

Commitment, courage, endurance. The esoteric choice can only ask everything of you. Choose or stop. Get off the train or endure and continue the journey with joy, enthusiasm, courage and a spirit of adventure.

Every good is within you: Look at your hands, strong or weak, they are your means and should be used to the maximum of their possibilities; look at your eyes, use them for everyone; and the same for your ears; your tongue. Believe, brother, and give all of yourself to the world.

Christ, who offered one of his bodies for everyone, upon the symbol of the cross of pain (which is renewal), reminds you that you must offer yourself for everyone. What other esoteric message is there? The *complete* offering of oneself, in order to be eternal and live within humanity.

How easy it is to forget others!

One thinks: "But why do I have to go on troubling myself for others if they don't give a damn about me?"

---

[10] Lanoo, Elder Brother, and Elder Sister are levels of initiation at Damanhur's School of Meditation.

It is a duty; it is a goal. The egotistical self must be subordinated to the good of others, by doing one's own duty.

Dusting the house is a duty, just as hoeing a field, building a house or working in an office, even if you know it is a useless job.

Be always seeking, in every moment; helping when help does not become charity, but communion of intent.

Accepting help when it is right means helping whoever helps you. But if you take advantage, with endless excuses, you will be nothing but a little worm.

Remember you can do a great deal and not only the things you like ...

When distress grips your throat and you feel useless, alone, without purpose, it is the moment for prayer. It will enable you to soak up strength, courage, and enthusiasm. It will instill you with cosmic and mysterious energies. It will show you the path to take.

Struggle, Initiate. Fight. Shout.

Destroy yourself and sacrifice yourself for your people. You will be humiliated and confused, because I love you. Treated badly and rebuked, we shall see if you can control your egotistical self.

The forces of time and space will tear you apart to strengthen you. When you declare your acceptance of the tests your every weak point will be touched.

Why all this? For HOPE.

Great, sublime, marvelous Hope!

The longing for a cleaner tomorrow, by means of today and now. I Hope.

Here is one of the greatest gifts of the human race: In spite of your hopelessness – which means, precisely, "no hope" – there exists in you the immortal seed of Hope.

Hope made and will make Humankind a harmonious being, in its place at the side of God.

To Believe, to have Faith, and to Hope!

To do everything with the inner drive that says to us: "Go ahead. Hope. Even if you don't know exactly what in."

What is there in the casket? And in the blue valley? And inside every one of us? What is that secret certainty in something indefinite but sure that we call Hope? Is it perhaps the ancestral memory of the nobility of our human species?

As Consciousness, oh Lanoo, I reply to you: "YES!"

You feel and know, believe and want to believe.

It is true. Humankind had a great part of the universe to itself – a great and glorious empire. Everything was harmonious and life was respected in all its forms.

Then the joint forces of the Apocalypse shook everything that was. And there emerged a New Creation.

Humanity – imprisoned and lobotomized – kept inside itself only the secret, the great force of Hope. That force that makes us fight our bestiality and allows us to prepare our ground and make ourselves fertile, with the goal of bringing about the Resurrection of the New Human Being, the Evolved Human Being, as described in the *I Ching*.

Even the society this New Human Being lives in is a new society.

The fundamental principle is the development of self-sufficient individuals, capable, that is, of taking care of themselves. Men and women who decide to be social individuals, not because they are obliged to, but out of Consciousness or, at least, free choice.

They will pay their debt of Consciousness working for the society that has set them free, by their own choice.

They will develop their own abilities to the maximum. They will not seek a specialization in one particular job, but will be able to do everything. Of course, if they are drawn in a special way to some particular job, they will be encouraged as much as possible to do the work most suited to them, that being wholly to the advantage of the Community.

The New Humans live – and used to live – in Intentional Communities, made up of single people and family organizations.

Every single person and family has their private vital space (home), because nobody is able to lead for long a Community life that is "too communal."

The children in this Community are everyone's, and it is the duty of everybody to do everything possible to improve the Knowledge of every one of the children. The families are composed of a man and a woman, who out of free choice decide to live together and to have children. Planning for children depends on the whole Community's being able to support them up to the age of independence, without excessive burdens on the Community itself.

As a social rule, marriages between individuals in the Community are for chosen periods (3-5-10-20 years and so on). Nothing prevents, other than serious reasons, the separation of the members of each family before the expected period, which is renewable.

The individuals of the Community – who are all equal – are expected to be self-sufficient and responsible, and to conduct themselves in a manner that does no harm to the Community as a whole.

This, however, does not mean that within the village (200-250 individuals maximum), one can make love at random. And the mature individuals of a Community constituted in such a manner know this ...

The Community, which is self-sufficient from the point of view of its energy supply and food, is composed of a fixed number of individuals.

Above this number, other villages are organized. The villages trade with one another for their unique products and services, those which are not essential for their lives. The villages with fields nearby will work them, and in exchange they will receive other products from other villages.

Upon reaching a certain age, the young people will move in order to complete their work-studies in other Communities, with the purpose of bringing a continual "fresh breath" to every village and to spread new ideas and visions of the world. Thus, there will never be excessive cultural distance among Communities, and they will encourage one another to constantly reach higher levels of development.

Even wars, in a world of the Age of Aquarius, will be overcome, because there would be no motive for war. Languages and ways of living will be shared by everyone, without violence.

Representatives of every Community will form regional councils, and they in their turn will be part of continental and world assemblies. This is how I see a world in the harmonious post-industrial Age of Aquarius. Very advanced and refined technologies will develop, suited to the Advanced Human Being, who will make use of them without ever depending on them.

This is a concise synthesis of the organization of the evolved planets. And also the kind of life that was led on our world a very, very long time ago.

Why did it come to an end?

Because humans mistakenly believed that weapons and defense were needed. And the earth, perhaps, aroused the greed and envy of others less evolved – the "Barbarians."

The path that will bring our planet back to being harmonious, clean and at peace, passes through the creation of self-sufficient Communities. They are creative, full of fantasy if we like, but above all formative for our children.

We still will need "imposed hierarchies," like courts of "law" and other such barbarities. But maybe not so our grandchildren, if we really work for them.

We shall work not for ourselves, as I have already said, but for others. Also for those who are to come.

One does not leave one's apartment full of rubbish and poisons, saying: "Who cares? My children can deal with it when they come to live here." Rather, one tries to leave the house spick and span. This is how it is for our planet at present. We musn't be destructive barbarians any more, but refined and evolved Initiate beings.

Thus the co-coordinators of the Communities, the so-called "heads," will be trained to manage the "Community Company" on the basis of their intelligence and ability.

Today, to hear that in a "free and democratic" country even a road-sweeper can become the head of a nation – with all due respect for this important job – makes me afraid. Would we let a competent road-sweeper become the manager in charge of a large industrial company? With his training, how long do you think the business would last?

Let us begin now to create this new and ancient society within ourselves. Let us create it with our thought, and then let us lay down the bricks.

The most important point of all, however, relates to the individuals: How to change them? How to purify ourselves? How to re-introduce a harmonious and mystical society?

A union between Gods and Humankind, with the power of thought and of magic joined to the simpler forces of the physical world. A communion of the practical, spiritual, and DIVINE.

Brother, have you renewed yourself? In times of distress have you remembered to pray?

Do you believe, brother, in yourself? Do you believe in our ideas? Do you have trust? Do you want to play out this life in the best possible way? Or do you want to waste it at the bar, at the movies, in those places where others provide an illusion – your fiction and theirs?

Perhaps now, this moment, you feel strong. But when the cock has crowed, perhaps you too will have betrayed yourself. And me.

It seems that betrayal is a human habit. Fear of what others will think makes one betray. "Me, him? Never saw him, never knew him."

Thus it has been and, when push comes to shove, it will still be so again ... until the destruction of *the* symbol.

How many times in the past, due to human wretchedness and cowardice, has suffering been centered on one person alone!

The sacrifice of Christ could have been karmically subdivided among many. But it was not to be ...

Better to close one's eyes and guiltily say: "Let others do it. Come what may, so long as it does not affect me."

What is to come will affect everyone.

Who will be Initiate enough to share this burden?

The days fly swiftly by. Time does not wait for us. How many moments of time are we able to catch? Tomorrow will always be what we decide today.

Are we so weak we have to delegate suffering?

Fine. The love of Consciousness is big enough to contain it, and so shall it be if you want. Don't cry then, over spilt Consciousness, but work every instant inside yourselves to have a little Consciousness to share.

Brothers, you have a goal in life. You are not without ideals.

And remember: On the esoteric path, even though the goals in your mind might be clear, you will not manage to realize them, because you will always discover goals much, much vaster and more important than you can imagine.

Gather and direct your energies with a prayer of weaving, with meditation and reinforcing the archetypes.

Offer and give yourselves as a present to God.

Resolution and modesty, courage and sensitivity, commitment and love.

With a "cocktail" like that you cannot fail. Unless you desire failure. If you could only see how your thought creates, oh Lanoo!

And how far reaching is your mind, which you consider small and weak! Just as the bear, who hugging a tree pulls it up by the roots, doesn't know its own strength, so you, Initiate, do not realize yours. You have powerful means to grow, but it takes your WILL.

How difficult it is to overcome laziness! True? You can pray, make vows, set yourself tasks, commit yourself to a thousand different disciplines (for example, thinking well of others). There are those who have taken vows of chastity for fixed periods, to gather their own energies and divine energies ... and that has been granted them. Everything is granted if the commitment is genuine and sincere.

Please, do not make "vows" because it is trendy, or because the others do it. Do what you feel. One's own duty carried out with commitment and integrity, even if it is then objectively not worth a great deal, is more valuable than an important task done half-heartedly.

Enjoy what you do! Remember that the esoteric choice goes beyond your present life.

As already in the past, you will reincarnate wherever necessary, and you will work together again. Study carefully these simple written words of mine. The use and application of lateral thinking will ensure that you are able to draw notable benefit from them.

Remember, Initiate: With my physical disappearance nothing changes. I shall continue to work with you and follow you, reprove, reward and encourage you. You will not get rid of me even when I'm dead! (Unless that is what you want, of course.)

I like my job; however it is always relative to the class I find myself in. I don't enjoy teaching in a classroom of immature slackers, but I give everything to pupils who ask for everything. So wish for everything!

I also like sensitive pupils who understand when I am tired, who don't just try to suck without ever digesting what I have given them.

What use is it "going up" if the stairs behind you are falling apart? What sort of passageway are you preparing for others? I have fallen, and died so many times on the stairs.

And I have died as a martyr and an assassin. As a scapegoat and blessed by the people. As someone condemned to death for the worst crimes.

I have died suffocated and squashed, swiftly and slowly, peacefully and painfully.

To conclude: I have died and I have renewed myself and I have risen again. How many times! How many! The return of Consciousness after switching off the Light!

And I have one great wish (in human terms). I would like to be able to tell you EVERYTHING.

I would like to talk to you about my secrets – everything that my experience has accumulated in every physical and non-physical science.

Maybe you can prepare yourselves sufficiently to hear them without being shocked!

Maybe you can save yourselves many lives and many deaths!

Maybe some of you in this lifetime will attain Realization!

Lastly, I pray that your Resurrection will happen in this era, which many scriptures call – and which is in fact – the "End Times."

The Master has spoken, and it is far into the night. The fire is glowing embers, and the stars wink shiny and bright.

The silence upon one's Consciousness allows one to clearly distinguish the sounds of the night.

Already during the day, comments made under someone's breath have split the Community in two.

Some want to crucify the Bearer of Hope, because he is only a charlatan who keeps them up late at night and in the morning everyone is tired. Those who think too much don't work hard enough, and winter is no joke ... forget about words!

On the other hand, some believe and have hope. They are beginning to understand and fight for awareness.

It is the choice between being ephemeral or eternal.

You – who are you with?

EPILOGUE

Light, we need Light. Every sign reminds us of this. Time goes by, the message does not grow old.

The Lords of Time, beyond the Doors, are watching Humankind with acute attention: They need to see if the patient is making any signs of recovery ... or not.

And yet we all have been little ones, children attentive to what the world was telling us. Why, growing up, do we forget about it? Perhaps salvation is only for the young?

No, it is for all who understand – for those who realize that they were conditioned too much during their childhood, those who were deluded into believing that "growing up" means reaching an age where one has to be cunning to fit in and avoid dangers, wary of the bad surprises that life brings.

Do not forget the freshness of our children, being children ourselves. Whoever said that the ages of man are to be so sharply divided?

Perhaps you were too influenced by the idea that play is something for little ones and no longer appropriate for mature adults. Did a great sage tell you that?

Or was it rather one of those many, too many ideas that parents pass down without ever having questioned them?

Once you are mothers and fathers, will you too instill those ideas in the minds of your children?

Growing does not necessarily mean defending oneself. It is the weak that need protection; the strong have no need to show their claws.

Is your society perhaps one where everyone snarls at each other to make their worth felt? Change it. Don't limit yourselves to complaining about it and then conforming to fit in.

Be pure, with healthy, clear ideas. Learn to be unafraid of the powers of those who shout the loudest. This way you will be invincible. Do not have any attachment – no one can steal the things you are not holding (but which you treat with respect).

Does this seem to you a message out of the world, out of time? Perhaps it is because you cling too much to the wings of the theatre where you are acting. Do you remember that it is all pretend?

Wake up, look around, you were hypnotized! For too many years you have played at being serious adults, and now you have forgotten that you were on stage for a performance, and nothing more.

An attentive audience, outside of your humanity, has been observing you during the entire show. I wanted to say "inhuman," but perhaps the term "superhuman" is more appropriate.

Beings with great, attentive minds and very subtle senses have judged you, have compared the script with your ability to act out the character you are now bringing to life. Beware that exaggerating makes you lose credibility! If your character takes you over, you are no longer a committed actor, but rather a madman!

Where is the boundary between interpretation and excessive internalization? A mediumistic trance has you lend your body to a character who has become more alive than you, yourself, the actor?

So strong as to put the more authentic part of your personality in second place? So deluded as to fuse you with the shadow?

Have you confused your real self with the mask, not even so amusing, which you now wear from habit?

Well then, dear friend, remember every now and then that you are always human, as children as well as adults. Remember that the difference between youth and physical maturity is an illusion, like measuring time with a clock. A convention, an agreement, a habit born so long ago that we have lost our memory of its origin.

So sit down by that fire on the beach, unafraid. Don't worry about dirtying your trousers on the sand; no one will tell you off when you get home (and if this is the thought bothering you, you have reached an all-time low).

Not only do you consider yourself an adult because you remind yourself of rules a child would never think of, you elevate the rules to avoid something that would give you pleasure, life, growth ... and get you away from that squalid character who you insist on acting out (somewhat dully), and who usually passes unnoticed.

In short, it is not good to always play the part of the villain in the film. Every now and again, put yourself in the shoes of the simple man, the good man (which in reality you are).

Look at others with curious eyes, without fear. Nobody will force you to buy anything. Come here, and talk. Don't immediately put a label on what you hear.

We have caught some good fish; there's some for you too. Sit down, there's definitely too much for us fishermen, and tomorrow it will be spoiled. Indeed, how do I convey this simple invitation without your immediately suspecting some plot to your detriment? I swear no one will ask anything of you. If you like, sit freely with us and chat awhile, otherwise do whatever you please.

Here we don't talk about sports, I warn you in advance. Nor do we wish to turn you into a proselyte, asking you to hand over money for some deserving cause. Since you are hesitating, I seriously doubt that anyone deserves that money more than you.

If you hesitate, you are *really* needy.

Here, take some of this fish and a bit of bread. It's good, homemade in a lovely wood oven only this morning. I've told you, it doesn't cost anything. It's not a promotional sale. No, we are not giving away coupons. I'm sorry, it is not a gathering sponsored by your favorite brand of nappies.

No sir, it is not the after-dinner drink you like so much that has organized this gathering, or the committee of this pleasant little seaside town. For postcards and coconuts it is further on, near that kiosk ... can you see?

We are here among ourselves to talk about LIFE!

Not about your very interesting trip to the Congo, or about your war memories, or about when you were twenty. Sorry, but we shall not even talk about women, cars, favorite brand of beer, interesting or boring jobs.

You say there's nothing else to talk about? That nothing else comes to mind as a topic of conversation?

Pity. I could find two or three little things to say.

In other words, whoever would like to, sit down and don't give me any more trouble ...

What say you, Master OroCritshna? Was it not alright, my little introduction? How should I do it then, when I set off and go around the world speaking of what you have allowed me to reveal?

You always say that there is little time, that the years are about to end, and that there are now few places left on the road for humanity.

Why should I have any more patience? Precisely because I'm too impatient?

If *you* say so, I believe. You, I obey.

From what I understood, when I used to sit around your fire, I have done nothing else but prepare myself for this earthly journey. My Master, I have been exerting myself in every way to put into practice what was revealed to me.

Hence, I shall be more patient.

Shall I yet be present then ... one day ... at the meeting of the two Great Deities who speak of Humankind, so as to understand properly?

What shall I do? Shall I use my voice in magical language to enter into contact and be present in their thoughts?

I shall do thus ...

I am you, Master. The body you will wear, a new name, Vadusfadam, child of the magical language.

I well remember your words, your teaching – within me and now, mine. And I shall give myself to those who will come.

I do not know if, as a guide on the path, on the road, I shall be right, perfect as you want me to be. But having you within me, it will be difficult to go wrong.

Follow me always, Master.

Even now that your body gets ready to leave.

Look, the celestial ship has come down!

Ah, if my friends could only see it! Only me did you want for this farewell, my Master?

Yes, I know that when I want to depart or when I am tired, I too shall be able to summon the ship.

And I also know that your work is never ended, now that you will sleep and your spirit will be awakened in me, forever present.

Of course I remember where the replacement bodies are. All these reminders and recommendations are unnecessary; after all, it is you who is leaving, not me. You say it is not so?

By the way, into what time shall I have to go? This ticket? Thank you. It is the number-sound of the time wave I shall inhabit very soon.

Good, then. I never liked farewells. In fact, not even a "see you later."

However, are you really sure to have chosen me and that down there – in that time – I shall have to choose others?

The last, the first ... pay no attention. Every now and then I can't help frowning a little.

So little time, so many things to be done ...

Yes, yes, don't remind me of the urgency, *et cetera*, *et cetera*. I know the whole story: a bet with the Lord Colleagues of the Council.

According to us, humanity can make it; according to them, it cannot. By now, it is a patient in a "terminal state," as they say down there where I am going.

Such is the fear of the word death. It must be a fine place, for sure! For sure, it is as they say, "damned."

In short, I am not a child any more ... Oops!

Sorry, it is just a manner of speaking ...

So then go, while I get ready to travel down there, to that place some history books still hint at.

Are we ready? So then, with you ...

And with YOU!

ABOUT THE AUTHOR

OBERTO *"Falco"* AIRAUDI

Oberto Airaudi is Damanhur's Spiritual Guide. His teachings encourage the awakening of the inner master through study, experimentation, overcoming dogmatic attitudes, and the complete expression of individual potential.

Born in 1950 in Balangero, Italy (near Turin), Mr. Airaudi is a philosopher, healer, writer, and painter. He is constantly involved in research into cutting-edge therapeutic applications, the arts and new sciences. In accordance with the Damanhurian custom of being called by animal names, Mr. Airaudi also uses the name of "Falco" (Falcon).

He chose this name to honor Horus, symbol of the divine principle to be awakened inside every human being and the cosmic God of the New Millennium.

From a very early age, Falco manifested a clear spiritual vision and the gift of healing. He committed to develop these gifts through constant and exacting experimentation, outside of traditional academic institutions. His spiritual and personal growth continued over the years via incessant studies, journeys of research, the awakening of his memories, the development of artistic skills, and the rediscovery of ancient knowledge.

In 1975, Falco founded the Horus Center in Turin. It was the first seed of a Mystery School and a community, and from its activities the Federation of Damanhur developed.

Damanhur was born to realize the dream of a society based on optimism and the idea that human beings can be the masters of their own destiny, without having to depend on other forces outside themselves. Indeed, the basis of Falco's vision is the belief that every human being participates, through conscious interactions with others, to awaken a divine nature within themselves. As a result, Damanhur is a society in constant evolution and transformation, based on the exaltation of diversity. Its social, political, and philosophical systems are always in flux.

Falco is a remarkably reserved person, and he has no decision-making role within the political or social structure of Damanhur, which is directed by elected bodies. If asked, he is always available to cooperate with the Federation's Guides, who are elected by the citizens.

About Damanhur

Founded in 1975, the Federation of Damanhur is an Italian eco-society based upon ethical and spiritual values. Damanhur has about 1,000 citizens and extends over 500 hectares of land throughout the Valchiusella region, at the foothills of the Piedmont Alps.

Damanhur is approximately 90% self-sustainable, with more than 80 businesses that foster agricultural and economic independence. Damanhur has a Constitution, complementary currency system, daily newspaper, art studios, centers for research and practice of medicine and science, open university, and education for children from elementary through middle school.

Damanhur promotes a culture of peace and equitable development through solidarity, volunteerism, respect for the environment, art, and social and political engagements. Courses and events are open to the public year round, and it is possible to visit for short periods as well as longer stays for study, vacation, or regeneration.

Damanhur's Temples of Humankind – often called the "Eighth Wonder of the World" – comprise an extraordinary underground network of chapels dedicated to the reawakening of the divine essence in every human being. The art studios that contributed to the stained glass, mosaics, and frescoes in the Temples are located at Damanhur Crea, a center for innovation, wellness, and research, which is open to the public every day of the year.

Damanhur operates additional centers in Italy, Europe, Japan, and the United States. Damanhur also collaborates with other international organizations engaged in the social, civic, and spiritual development of the planet.

Damanhur has received world-wide recognition for its innovative and inspiring approach to life. Since 1988, Damanhur has been a member of the Global Eco-Villages Network, and in 2005 it received a United Nations sustainability award. In 2007, *EnlightenNext* magazine voted Damanhur the most evolved community on earth.

Please visit the Damanhur website for additional information and directions on how to visit the community.

www.Damanhur.org

ABOUT THE PUBLISHER

The Truth

The founders of The Oracle Institute are gravely concerned that the greatest crisis facing humanity is the resurgence of religious intolerance perpetrated in the name of God. We chose the Pentacle as our icon because, to us, this symbol represents the emerging spiritual unification of the five primary religions: Hinduism, Judaism, Buddhism, Christianity, and Islam. We believe the time has come for humanity to shed archaic belief systems and prepare for the next phase of our collective spiritual evolution.

The Love

The Oracle Institute promotes a process of soul growth which includes study, worship, meditation, and good works through application of the Golden Rule: the "Eleventh Commandment" brought by Jesus. When we earnestly strive to perfect ourselves, practice compassion toward others, and assume responsibility for the health of our planet, we help birth a new spiritual paradigm.

The Light

Many people are now ready to manifest "heaven on earth" – the prophesied era of abundance, peace, and harmony foretold by the prophets of every religion and the elders of every indigenous wisdom culture. To that end, The Oracle Institute offers interfaith books, spirituality classes, civics seminars, health and mindfulness programs, and holistic products designed to foster the quest for spiritual enlightenment.

We Invite You to Join Us
on Our Journey of

TRUTH, LOVE, and LIGHT

Donations may be made to:

THE ORACLE INSTITUTE
A 501(c)(3) Educational Charity

*An Advocate for Enlightenment and
A Vanguard for Spiritual Evolution*

1990 Battlefield Drive
Independence, Virginia 24348
www.TheOracleInstitute.org

All donations and proceeds from our books and classes are used to
further our educational mission and to build the Peace Pentagon,
an interfaith and social justice center in Independence, Virginia.

ALSO BY THE ORACLE INSTITUTE PRESS

Dying to Learn: First Book of the Initiate
By Oberto "Falco" Airaudi of Damanhur

Reborn to Live: Second Book of the Initiate
By Oberto "Falco" Airaudi of Damanhur

Seven Scarlet Doors: Third Book of the Initiate
By Oberto "Falco" Airaudi of Damanhur

Bral Talej Divination Cards
By Shama Viola and Oberto "Falco" Airaudi

Trusting Doubt:
A Former Evangelical Looks at Old Beliefs in a New Light
By Valerie Tarico, Ph.D.

Deas and Other Imaginings:
Ten Spiritual Folktales for Children
Written by Valerie Tarico, Ph.D. and Illustrated by Tony Troy

The Truth: About the Five Primary Religions
Book I of The Oracle Institute Foundational Trilogy

The Love: Of the Fifth Spiritual Paradigm
Book II of The Oracle Institute Foundational Trilogy

The Light: And the New Human
Book III of The Oracle Institute Foundational Trilogy

www.TheOracleInstitute.org